NO
SHAME

NO SHAME

How to drop the guilt ... from someone
who's learned the f**king hard way

LAURA BELBIN

**EBURY
SPOTLIGHT**

1

Ebury Spotlight, an imprint of Ebury Publishing
20 Vauxhall Bridge Road
London SW1V 2SA

Ebury Spotlight is part of the Penguin Random House group of companies
whose addresses can be found at global.penguinrandomhouse.com

First published by Ebury Spotlight in 2022

www.penguin.co.uk

A CIP catalogue record for this book is available from the British Library

ISBN 9781529148411

Typeset in 11.5/19.3pt ITC Galliard by Jouve (UK), Milton Keynes
Printed and bound in Great Britain by Clays Ltd, Elcograf S.p.A.

The authorised representative in the EEA is Penguin Random House
Ireland, Morrison Chambers, 32 Nassau Street, Dublin D02 YH68

Penguin Random House is committed to a
sustainable future for our business, our readers
and our planet. This book is made from Forest
Stewardship Council® certified paper.

To you, to us, for all survivors.

CONTENTS

CONTENTS

CHAPTER 1

Triggered

Hello, my name is Laura, and in 2021 I experienced the biggest mental breakdown of my life. I am writing this book because it feels like something that will feed my soul, heal some wounds and hopefully help some of you realise your own strength. Some of you might not know me, but I am a public figure/entertainer/comedian/realist who frequents social media channels like Facebook and Instagram as Knee Deep In Life. My main goal is to poke fun at the ridiculous life expectations that are plastered all over social media while also speaking passionately about mental health, female empowerment and how fucking shit life can be sometimes.

I have suffered with mental health problems for all of my life; I have lived with anxiety and undiagnosed PTSD, which has been incorrectly labelled as depression. I have been forced to face a lot this year and accept something I've denied myself for the whole of my life: help.

In January 2021, I was like most parents, struggling like fuck to cope with the pressures of homeschooling children. I was struggling with the level of entrapment life felt like back then, and I really, really fucking needed a break. My husband, Steve, would bugger off to work each day, something I resented him for because it seemed like a trip to the Bahamas in comparison to teaching my 10-year-old his 7 times table when even I didn't fucking know my 7 times table. I was like most people, well and truly at the end of my rope, but I just didn't realise. I didn't realise, in my ignorance, that we were all feeling it, because it felt and looked like everyone else didn't mind staying in, teaching their children and doing Zoom parties with their mates. I thought I was the only one who felt like real life was so far off that I just couldn't stand how slowly everything was going. I spoke to people, hoping they could offer some kind of reassurance, but they all seemed to be trudging along, and I felt like I was four steps behind them, being dragged along backwards by my toenails.

I had put the expectation of being a mum, wife and teacher so high in the sky, I wasn't actually able to get onto the ladder to reach it. I'd set my standards so high for what was personally achievable that even if I'd been the shining example of a mother and wife, I still wouldn't have managed it. I was, in short, drowning but felt like I couldn't admit that because then I'd really be failing at everything.

Then Steve had to self-isolate and I thought, *YAY, he will be home, he can help me!! We can do this together. He might have Covid but fuck it, that surely seems easier than living with our children all the time on my own with no adult to talk to.* Well, I spent the 10 days he isolated for with a rat up my arse. I thought he was doing a better job than me, I thought he was trying to get one over on me whenever he taught the kids as I sat on my arse staring at the carpet, and I cried A LOT for no real or good reason.

Two days before he was due to go back to work, I thought, *I am fucking done!!* I couldn't do this any more, juggling my own job, the kids, trying to make some kind of money and also being funny for everyone on the internet when everything in my life didn't feel particularly funny.

I realised I needed something to help. I went to the doctor with a stomach ache, and left with a prescription for antidepressants because I realised I couldn't go on like I had been.

That night, I didn't sleep. I panicked and took a migraine tablet; logic told me that was the only thing in the house that would make me sleep. NOPE. Didn't sleep. So, the following morning I declared to Steve, 'I am definitely starting the antidepressants.' I took them, and Steve fucked off to work. *Great. I am now taking something that'll make all my problems disappear!!* HAHAHAAAAAA, I know; I can already hear you all saying, 'WHAT THE FUCK?? Tablets just take away all your problems??' Short answer is no, they don't, but back then I honestly thought any mental health issue is fixed by taking a tablet. No other work required.

I didn't sleep; in actual fact, I went into full-blown shit-level stations.

This is bad, I thought. *I am going to die in the space of 48 hours.*

I can remember well the moment where everything changed. I was driving my kids out to take them for a walk, and I realised 30 minutes in I was going in the wrong direction. I asked them if we could just go home because Mummy didn't feel good. They obviously did the kid thing and said, 'Shit no, we want our walk!!' I felt too weak and broken to even argue the toss over it. So I took them. I arrived in the car park, turned off the car and messaged Steve, saying, 'I need you. I can't do this alone this time, you need to take some time off from work to help me.'

I had suffered with postnatal depression after having both of my children, in 2011 and 2015. I had
taken medication in 2015, which had had the worst
side effects, but since then, Steve had continued to go
to work and I had continued to manage life at home,
but only by a thread. That day in the car park I felt like
the thread had finally pinged and I wasn't going to
manage it this time.

Steve organised to be at home from work for a
week, but I steadily got worse. I lay in bed, unable to
sleep, completely exhausted and totally alone, crying,
as my children slowly lost their mum into an abyss of
panic. On the Friday I contacted my doctor's surgery,
begging for sleeping tablets – something I had previously been given when I had suffered with postnatal
depression. They played down my situation and said it
was because I was close to my period. They reluctantly
gave me three tablets and told me to space them out
because they were highly addictive.

I didn't.

I took the maximum dose; I didn't sleep.

Over that weekend I called out of hours, spoke to
mental health nurses and was prescribed different
medication to help me. None of it did.

I was given something designed to help with anxiety and make me drowsy.

I slept for an hour.

It was 11.30pm on a Sunday evening on the last weekend of January when I came downstairs to Steve and said, 'I can't do this any more.'

Not in an 'I'm bored, let's do something different' kind of way; instead it was more 'I am going to end my life.' In four short days of asking Steve to help me, I was on my knees, on the floor, as he held me and I sobbed like a scared small child, as I kept saying over and over, 'I am going to kill myself.'

Steve was terrified; to be honest, so was I. I have never, ever felt so out of control in my entire life; I have never felt more selfish in my wish to leave everyone else behind either. I stopped caring about how it could make anyone else feel, including my kids, and I just wanted to die. I honestly couldn't imagine another hour of my life feeling that terrible.

I called 999 and I begged, I sobbed and I pleaded for someone to help me because I was going to take all the medication in the house. Steve sat there, next to me, completely silent. I can't imagine how utterly shit this must have been for him.

At 5.30am an ambulance arrived for me. I sat on the sofa, rocking, scratching my head, rubbing my legs and sobbing as my kids slept. I believe I was having an adverse reaction to the anxiety medication I had taken that night, which was only adding to my issues. The ambulance crew told me there was nothing that could be done to help me, that I just needed to wait until my doctor's surgery opened the following morning and speak to them then. That was it; that's all I had. My saviour didn't exist; there was no place to go to help me get better.

They then listened to my heart, and picked up an irregularity: it was skipping a beat and it was something I felt constantly. They took me into hospital, only based on the fact I had a heart irregularity. I could almost sense the fact the ambulance crew felt helpless seeing someone so broken and having to walk away from the scene having done nothing to help, because threatening to end my life wasn't enough to actually take me anywhere. I was so exhausted. I had nothing left to give, I just sat in the ambulance looking at the floor as the ambulance driver took my details and social services were contacted because my children's mother (me) had threatened to end her life.

That is where I had got to. I was that mum who now would have social services involved with her children because she just couldn't cope. I felt like it was such a direct attack on my parenting, even though above all else all the ambulance crew were doing was quite rightly protecting my children because I was clearly in crisis.

That morning our youngest son came into our bedroom and asked where I was. Steve, who had probably had one hour's sleep, had to tell him Mummy had needed to take a little trip to hospital and would be back soon. He lay on my side of the bed and cried and sobbed. He begged Steve to go and get me; the heartache of that moment will probably never leave me – no, I wasn't there to experience that first hand, but it doesn't make it any less painful to know. My breakdown meant I just couldn't even begin to manage my kids' needs as well as my own. I am always going to be their mum and knowing that moment destroyed them emotionally will never be something I can easily wash away.

I was given the once-over in hospital and told my heart was fine, that whatever was consuming me would be fine, and that I just needed to go back to my GP. They had tapped every vein in my body to get blood, I had threatened to kill myself and I was so exhausted

I wanted to die. But I was okay in a medical sense so apparently what I needed to do was simply go home and ride this out. What *was* 'this'? Medication side effects? Depression? Anxiety? Bipolar? Dissociative identity disorder (previously known as multiple personality disorder)? Honestly, I couldn't have told you because I didn't know; I just knew it was the very worst thing that was almost impossible to describe.

My GP gave me the strong sleeping tablets and I was reminded once again that their addictive nature meant I should only take them sparingly.

I DIDN'T.

I maxed the dose each night, and would wake up multiple times a night, panicking. I just felt completely out of control.

I just wanted to go back to the person I had been a week earlier. She was managing! What had happened?

I was triggered.

You see this word thrown around a lot; it can either be used as a way of explaining an emotion that isn't easy or it can be used in jest. I do both!! I can be the first person to take the piss out of myself using the throwaway line of being triggered but, in actual fact, it is a deeply personal way to describe something pretty fucking awful.

I say all of this as the person still insanely ashamed that I fell THAT HARD from life, from grace (never had any grace), and came slapping so hard against the ground the thud was felt within the whole community of people who love me.

In the wake of this situation, two children – who'd had a mum that cooked dinner and took them out for muddy walks – were left all of a sudden with a woman who did nothing because everything was exhausting.

I was urged by my doctor to start a form of therapy. I found someone relatively cheap in my local area who described herself as a counsellor who specialised in trauma. Well, this experience alone was pretty traumatic so I thought she fit the profile.

I ended up seeing her twice a week and I seemed to fall deeper into a rabbit hole of previous traumatic experience, which was only making me more panicked and scared. I truly felt, *This is it, this is my life now, and I don't have the luxury of coming back from this. I just have to live at this level of misery.*

I had reached a point in my life where I was no longer leaving the house. I removed all social media from my phone and completely stopped communicating with everyone. My friends would message Steve, asking for updates, as he tactfully tried to explain:

'Laura is fucked right now; I don't know what to tell you.'

I didn't eat, I lost weight and, every time Steve left the house, I would hold on to his bedtime T-shirt like a small child with their comfort blanket.

I didn't trust myself. Steve was too scared to trust me. I sat there, desperately feeling like a complete failure.

Why me? I thought. *This isn't fair, I don't deserve this. I didn't do anything wrong . . .*

Those words haunt me because, even now, I still feel a level of complete disbelief that I could have been so ignorant about my own mental health that I didn't get help sooner.

Roll on six weeks. I was seeing the counsellor twice a week and feeling like I was surrounded by my past and unable to even remotely live in the present. At this time, I reluctantly spoke to my friend. She's a psychologist. I didn't want her to hear me so broken; I felt ashamed and humiliated that she would see me like that. She urged me to immediately stop seeing the counsellor because my trauma wasn't being managed effectively.

I trusted her. So I did as she advised and, through the recommendation of my beautiful friend, who will remain nameless to protect her own identity, I found my current therapist: a psychologist who specialises in trauma and practises EMDR, a form of therapy, which, albeit intense, has since worked for me. It has been the hardest slog of my life. I have cried in every session, I have refused to address multiple issues because, like some weird sticky glue, they seem to be stuck to my insides like a part of me that doesn't want to come undone because it could in turn undefine me.

Right, let me say this, which I have typed out and deleted multiple times because fear has got in the way of saying it out loud: I am a survivor of childhood sexual abuse. I am a survivor because I refuse to be a victim. I am a survivor because, even when I thought I would give up, I actually didn't. Something inside me said to keep going, even though there was a big part of me that was telling me to give up. I never did. It is really important that I note here before you go on that this wasn't abuse by a family member, but I was under six when it happened. While I could go into great detail over my age, and my family, I also want to respect the fact that this was a horrifically awful situation that rocked my whole family. I want to share my story, not someone else's account of it, and I want to be strong enough to know that this is mine to share. I don't have to hide it any more. I am speaking of this from a first-hand perspective as a survivor of childhood abuse who has found the bravery to use her voice and not include the voices or experiences of anyone else who was connected to the situation.

The direct result of all my breakdowns links back to the abuse I received as a child; this is the reason I live with PTSD and why I have carried trauma around like an old shopping bag I don't want to get rid of. It has defined many moments of my life, and I have wanted to talk about it so many times but never felt brave enough. I have thought endlessly about why I want to share it now. The simple answer is I was silenced by fear of speaking up for 37 years of my life, and I wonder who else is reading this, maybe suffering with mental health issues, with a backlog of trauma, who isn't aware that something that happened in their past is the reason they are plagued and wishes some-one would tell them they aren't alone. It is such a hard thing to begin to understand, the reasons why we suffer. Why we tick the way we do. Maybe some of you will have been through this journey already. You'll already understand why you have mental health issues; maybe you're like me and learning along the way? Either way, I think above all else, if you are reading this you know without a shadow of a doubt that you most definitely aren't alone.

I want to share this not to sell books, but because it is something I have felt the most shame over, that I have felt completely alone in and that I wished I could remove from my very existence, but I've realised I can't remove it. I need to make room for it; I need to allow that experience to be there, and know it was completely unfair, and disgusting, but I did survive it. I have been able to answer a lot of painful questions, all thanks to therapy. None of this is easy but I want it to be here. I need it to be here, without the fear of being accused of making it up, or over-dramatising it. I need it in this book because it is my reality and it goes some of the way to explaining why I have experienced what I have experienced without brushing it off as just 'mental health issues'. Like, my issues have a cause and a reason. I have denied that for all my life because I didn't want to admit my abuser had that much control over me. I have to say I loathe that this is the truth but, up until I hit rock bottom, there was a massive part of me that was completely controlled by the fear, rejection and abuse I received at the hands of another man. It will hurt everyone who knows me to read this; it hurts me too, but who do I hide this from? And why? To make it easier for my abuser? To make it easier for everyone else? I don't want to do that any more. I deserve more for myself, and so, while there are many factors that go into the reasons behind why I have been in crisis with my mental health, one of the biggest root causes will always come back to the physical and mental abuse I received as a child.

I have learned that, every time I have a child, my trauma response is triggered because, as a survivor of abuse, I feel such an overwhelming need to protect my babies and yet I've panicked because I have not understood what is happening in my body when I can't sleep, and I both want someone to take my babies away while also feeling so protective of them I would kill for them. I have felt the extreme highs and lows of emotions because my body was fighting to regulate itself. I have suffered panic where I have thought I would die, because I wasn't learning any techniques to save myself. I will never, ever be okay about the fact that the early days of motherhood were stolen from me because I hadn't addressed my childhood. That was my choice, albeit an uneducated one; I didn't acknowledge how powerful it had been. I refused to address it and buried it. However, you can only keep things buried for so long before they come bubbling to the surface, and mine has overspilled several times – each time worse than the last. My hope is by working as hard as I am at my own personal growth that I won't ever go to that rock bottom again.

I have put in place so many steps to build on my own personal strength that I hope I am able to always use my strategies to never let it happen again.

I don't even want to suggest or entertain the idea that, if I end up there again, I know how to get back, because I think that idea is utter bullshit. I just never again want to visit a place so dark and from where I didn't even realise it was humanly possible to make it back.

I did make it back, though, and I most definitely am a different person. I need to be to continue to survive life. We all hide truths; we don't have to expose everything, but sometimes there are things we feel are important enough to speak about. I want to talk about how real this is in my life, not that I just – boom! – one day got fixed, because that is unrealistic and completely not the truth. How does anyone just get fixed? Become trauma-free? Completely solve all their issues and feel happy all the time? That person isn't real.

I have always promised to be funny, but no one human being can effectively bring the funny in all moments without there being a huge detrimental impact to their own personal well-being. We aren't programmed robots who are set to experience a selective few emotions. We are all human; we are all capable of amazing and awful things. We all have the opportunity to be better, learn more and grow.

I understand this could be triggering for people to read; however, we can't escape the things we struggle with. Trying to avoid them actually makes them feel harder to manage, impossible to control and debilitating in their strength. I read this quote somewhere, which I will probably slaughter because I can't remember it exactly, but it went something along the lines of how the world can't be expected to manage your triggers, that you need to do that for yourself.

So, for instance, when I hear or witness something that sends my anxiety into overdrive, drops my intrusive thoughts in from a great height or makes my PTSD drop-kick me straight in the face, it isn't someone else's responsibility to manage that trigger. It isn't for them to silence themselves to soothe me; it's for me to learn to manage.

So, this will trigger someone with a response. Hopefully it'll give you a positive realisation that we can change our mindset. Triggered or not.

I was given this book deal straight after the release of my first book and I welcomed it with open arms. The opportunity to talk about female liberation and how infuriating it is that we lack so much equality. I wanted it to be a book about women and how we are expected to surrender to the idea of how we are limited to what we can do because we are women; I wanted to make sure we move forward united. I then had my breakdown and realised I couldn't talk about that stuff; as much as it is a passion and a drive in my life. The one glaring thing that came out of my breakdown was the importance to talk about the one thing I am dealing with at the moment, which is my mental health. I am a living example of how it really doesn't matter how far you go in life, you can sometimes be completely plagued by your own lack of self-esteem, and you can't move forward because you don't feel you belong in the rooms you're stepping into.

I don't particularly feel like I belong in the realms of being a writer, an author. I feel like an imposter, and yet here I am, typing away at another book. I am trying and working really hard at being a little more accountable for myself and also being a little prouder of how capable I am, as well as acknowledging how none of this 'just happens'. It does take work. Believe it or not, I'm writing this all myself, the dyslexic mum of two. No one is typing it for me and yet I'm still trying to figure out how I confidently accept I am the reason why good things happen to me. It isn't luck, it is talent and it is a whole lot of work. All these things are rarely spoken about because you are accused of being arrogant, but actually it's okay to work on saying those things out loud. So, allow me to conclude this with, no, this book isn't what was originally intended, and, yes, I am working on that old imposter syndrome and also on being proud that I am able to be honest enough about it.

I am not owning those words completely yet, but I am working on it. I am trying to figure out why I believe I am not deserving!

You see these quotes plastered all over social media saying, 'Read this out loud and in one month's time you'll have the money you always dreamed of.' Mate, if that was the case I'd be in a six-bed with four cars and a fucking chef, and no amount of me repeating it while I brush my teeth in the morning is going to change that. I can understand the meaning behind these things, they are basically saying you need to believe in yourself to see your full potential. I understand the premise of it and yet my thoughts still stand that I'm not going to become a fucking millionaire because I channelled my inner Oprah for four weeks. Everything takes work, it takes mental and physical work. I know this now more than ever. I can't sit around and work out which pill to take, the blue one or the red one. Might have worked for Keanu in *The Matrix* but it sure as fuck doesn't happen like that in real life. It is much slower, it is harder and you have to exhaust the mental patterns you have learned to play out in your head where you believe you aren't good enough to do something. I played out the idea of never leaving the house in the early part of last year, and it destroyed me. Being housebound, never taking my children out in the car again, never seeing them coming out of school – it broke me in two. I couldn't bear the life-limiting belief I had taught myself, which is that I can only do so much, and then allow fear to completely wipe out anything else I have to offer to the world.

I had to work really hard to come back from where I have been, and I have learned along the way that hard work was all down to me. Not Steve, not my friends or family. Me! I am my hero, I am my saviour, I am my rock and I had to stop and reject the idea of it being anyone else because that's all I ever offered myself as a reason to work at something in life. I had to do it to show them I could, to make them proud, to prove to them I was strong enough. I never, ever want to be that person again and being who I want to be is perfectly healthy.

This brings me on to something I feel is really important to address before I go any further.

HONESTY

I feel I owe you a level of honesty before you delve into this book and eat it up like a slice of cake over a coffee. I have read and continue to read books by men and women who tell you all the ways to save you from yourself. I want to do that, but, as I sit here at my dining room table – well past my kids' bedtime and yet they are still awake and annoying the shit out of me – I know the truth is I am imperfect and absolutely not owning all my shit. So I want to be honest and say this book is a take on what I want to give you, the reader, but also something I want to take for myself – I'm learning on the job, I guess. Does that make me a fraud? I fucking hope not. I think it more just proves the point I am always making, which is that we can all talk the talk, but that doesn't necessarily mean we walk the walk.

I have spoken so often in the past about how all you need to do is this one thing/these two things/a list of things to change how you see your world, and I have realised it's all a crock of shit because all that actually happens or what we all hope will happen from our words is that it makes people feel more enthusiastic about giving something a go. Has life in recent times – surviving a pandemic and living with children 24/7 – changed my perspective on what honesty looks like? Yes, and I think that has gone some of the way towards releasing some of the shame I have carried around with me for nearly all of my life. Admitting I was still struggling with the things I was telling other women to work through felt heavy and it felt like shit because I predominantly felt like I was utterly failing at every aspect of my life. How could I manage to give away such sound advice to others and keep none of it for myself while then expecting other women to follow it? How could I struggle so much with self-acceptance and yet have so many solutions for other women?

One of our problems with shame is our lack of ability to own it. Own who we are, in that moment, and let go of the ideas we are expected to have just because we are women, or because we are mums, or wives, or partners. This idea that we were designed to carry and birth children with zero impact on our self-esteem/worth and without a decline in our mental health. All these things – our bodies, our minds – are such precious things and yet we disregard them on a daily basis because they aren't where we would like them to be. I don't want to suffer with mental health problems, I want someone to take them away for me. I want it to feel less hard to keep myself together and to let go of the things that have plagued me enough to cause me three very big, scary breakdowns.

Before 2021, I truly believed my breakdowns were the direct result of having children. That definitely didn't fucking help, but I've since learned that a lot more than that went into them. I have had to fully accept myself – who I am as well as who I will always fight to be – no matter how hard I might try to push against my nature. Denying reality doesn't make it go away; it only makes it harder to smile through what feels like something exceptionally crushing.

I hate this idea that I need to be something and someone I am meant to be, because that something and someone is only ever for everyone else and never for me. The smile I paint on, it makes it easier for me to show my face in public, but if I actually wanted to cry instead and held it back, that would be because as a society we shame anything that doesn't fit within what we find comfortable. Examples of the things we do to make others feel comfortable are telling jokes, making others laugh, showing kindness, being generous, giving compliments. All those things go a long way towards making others like us, and feel safe around us, and we do them because we don't want to be rejected. We don't want to feel like the outcast for saying 'I feel this is too hard', or for sitting silently, not being the loud, bubbly one, or even just for crying because everything feels like too much. We deny ourselves because we worry about people avoiding us, or labelling us as 'unstable' or even 'weird'. All those things, though, they are natural, completely okay human feelings, which you, if you are even remotely normal, will actually experience at many points in your life. Yet it's not the norm to show them. The balance between being what everyone expects you to be and what you need to be for you is a fine line and sometimes feels a lot like juggling diarrhoea – in short, you don't balance it very well at all.

So, while I go off on one about why I want to be honest, it's because the human part of me needs to convey the fact I desperately want to get this completely right for you. I want you to read this book and think, *Wow, she fucking gets it!* But actually if I didn't give you the complete truth, which is that I'm learning with you, then I would only be continuing to be part of the problem, leading you to believe I know everything about how to manage shame, mental health and ultimate happiness. That's a wonderful idea we all think we will one day achieve, but it's more of a daily task of making sure we don't slip back to the negative way in which we used to live – and that even when we do in fact slip back, we forgive ourselves for it. I want this book to help you, but I don't want this book to make you feel like the end result is a million miles away. I want to hold your hand while you digest it and realise you aren't alone because I am there with you.

I am coming at you live and central from the strongest point I have managed to reach since having my breakdown one year ago, and I am promising you something I most definitely wouldn't have been able to give you two years ago, and that is a complete and open reality behind what I feel, and what has helped me, and how I see things. This is no one's gospel but my own and I hope it goes some of the way towards helping you figure out your own version of what you need in order to be mentally strong and less riddled with shame. My hope with this book is to give you a little insight into shame, what it looks like, how it feels and why, no matter how shitty it might feel, we all have it. I will break down the nitty gritty of boundaries and the beautifully challenging world of therapy. So buckle up, this is going to be a gloriously bumpy ride.

CHAPTER 2

Shame

Shame, shame, know your name. Do we own it? Being a woman, that is. Do we fuck! We live in fear of how we look, what we eat, how we age and what we do because society says women should look beautiful, never burp or fart in front of their partner and always suck like a hoover on demand.

The age-old debate – how to be the perfect woman?? Wow, 2022 and we're still churning out that same old shit. There are key points that show the difference between men and women and how we are seen by not only the opposite sex, but our peers too.

What does shame look like for women? To name a few examples . . .

- Guilt (tick)
- Poor self-esteem (tick)
- Negative self-chat (tick)

- Lacking motivation to improve your situation (tick)
- Blaming yourself (tick)
- Disassociation (tick)

According to the fabulous Brené Brown, men and women generally show shame in completely different ways, believe it or not. Men are more likely to show it outwardly in anger and aggression. Women are more likely to absorb and internalise it. In short, being a woman makes you more susceptible to a little-known case of the shames. No, I'm not saying men don't feel it too. Of course, it is part of the human condition we are taught to live by, but overall there is a clear difference in how we deal with that level of trauma. There is an expectation of men to be seen as a non-failure – the need to be good in bed, have a big dick, know what to do with it and be successful in their ability to hunt and gather – which can be pretty fucking overwhelming. Meanwhile women are desperately saying over and over, 'I'M FINE!! EVERYTHING IS JUST FINE!' as everything falls to fucking shit on the inside, because how can any good woman ever admit to feeling like they need time for themselves?? Or loving their body?? Or nailing being a parent when the constant fear of judgement from other mums is looming?!

That is exactly how I would like to describe shame. It is traumatic. No one says to their friend, 'Hey, I itched my piles the other day and one popped.' Why? Because they would feel embarrassed and the chances of the friend being visibly appalled or shocked would then make them feel ashamed. They would then internalise how it's very bad to speak up about things that might be happening in their own life. So we learn to be the less true, more watered-down version of ourselves to fit into this society.

That experience could be traumatic for either party involved: the person hearing it and the person saying it. We can't define shame by any one experience because it is completely unique to each person. Two people from completely different backgrounds could hear the same thing, said by the same person, in the same room, at the same time, and absorb that information differently. One person could come away feeling enlightened while the other is struggling with what they've just heard. That goes to show how huge the issue of shame is to tackle.

Here are just some of the things society makes us feel ashamed of as women:

- Women who sleep around – SLAG.
- Women with disability – incapable.
- Women who wear short skirts – putting them-selves at risk.
- Women who take antidepressants – unstable.

I mean, all of the above in my opinion is utter bullshit. I hate that any of these has to be a discussion point, yet imagine what it must feel like to the people who have to live with those labels. Yes, some of the above does apply to men, but the 'slag', the 'local bike' – do you hear men labelled with those tag lines? The odd time maybe, but – let's be fucking honest here! – those kinds of insults are predominantly aimed at women.

I have been medicated on and off throughout my adult life, not just with antidepressants but also anxiety medication and strong sleeping tablets. I have felt so crippled by people knowing this that, even when I have gone for appointments where they ask for current medication, I've pretended to not be on them and I haven't listed them. The fact I could have potentially risked my own well-being to hide the medication I was on to save face is pretty tragic, but imagine being that person with a long-standing relationship with highly addictive sleeping tablets and feeling every inch of the person's face look you up and down like you are a drug addict. OH the SHAMMMEEEE when you are the mum who shows up with a snazzy little bob, make-up on and wearing clean clothes. When you don't fit the stereotypical crack den type, and yet they assume you are as good as one for taking something they wouldn't ever dream of. To be honest, if I had a choice, neither would I, because weaning yourself off of said medication is no fucking walk in the park either. For the record, I wasn't addicted; but I don't know, maybe I was? I was solely dependent on them being in my house every day to make sure I slept at night and I didn't go a night without them for many, many months. Maybe that *is* a slight addiction . . . maybe I'll mention it to my therapist. THE POINT is I have stayed silent for the fear of other people's judgement and how they would treat me if they knew the truth. It also raises a very important point and that is we assume too much based on people's appearances. The mum with the snazzy bob and clean clothes would never be the drug user because according to society she is the stable one. I mean, what a crock of shit.

We are in an age where it is finally becoming more acceptable to be openly gay, trans, or even publicly carry the baggage of bipolar, depression or anxiety because more people are sharing their experiences, and yet we still live in such fear over who is watching us live our lives, and how we are being judged. We are all so proudly speaking up about our passions, our stories, and yet across the media we are still seeing victim blaming and misogyny.

We constantly tell ourselves we want to be different, we want change; we crave the unrealistic while kidding ourselves that it is completely achievable. The question always remains – why? Why do we continually do this to ourselves? How can we be so kind to others, and yet so toxic to ourselves?

I would like to take my coat of shame and hang it up on the peg. I would like to wash it off and leave it in the bath. I want to outrun it, but the reality is I can't run for shit and anyway, there is no outrunning something that has been there for generations upon generations. We are meant to stay ashamed, mainly because we have absolutely no idea as a society how to live without it. We judge everyone, we assume too much and know too little.

Even down to the single mum, we judge her! Maybe not you and me specifically, but as a society we judge the mum who lives in a council flat with three kids from three different dads, with bad mental health and with previous partners who beat her. We shame her by saying things like, 'Well, it's her own fault for getting into such terrible relationships.' No one asks to be hit! No one asks to be skint. Yeah, okay, there are opportunities to better ourselves but who the fuck are we to sit there and say she is shameful for not managing life how we expect her to? That shame is fucking crushing, and she feels it. Every single day she leaves her home and walks down the road in shoes that have seen better days, a pushchair and children screaming in tow. She feels our shame, and it's devastating because how is that woman meant to trust life, boyfriends, a future, when we can't even give her the respect she deserves?

This woman I just described is one example, but we can change the story and make it fit any one of us. It is the woman who lost weight and gained it back, the mum who is in an abusive relationship, the career woman who chose not to have children, the teenager who has panic attacks while everyone is telling her she has no reason to feel that way.

Like, it is every single one of us. We wear that coat of shame, but the fur is made of a different story, and lined with a different life. It starts from the moment we take our first breath. We are fucked from every angle because this has been happening since the dawn of time. Not even that long ago, women were tortured and labelled as witches at the mere whiff of rebellion of the patriarchy. (According to these strange-as-fuck times, so-called witches could even make a man's penis disappear . . . Whatever they were smoking I think I might want a go.)

It may seem far-fetched that such public shaming would happen today, but is it really? Our cancel culture is strong, and it has the same level of power that burning someone at the stake did. Many people have taken their lives as a direct result of online abuse, or they have been plagued with a long list of mental health issues such as anxiety because they've been too scared to leave their house in case someone hurts them. That witch . . . she isn't too far from our society, and she will be burned at any sniff of indifference to what she chooses to put out to the world.

I am all for justice but there is a fine line between that and getting something between your teeth and wanting to watch someone burn because of envy or hatred. That isn't healthy.

Why haven't I spoken up sooner about being a survivor of abuse? Because I have felt so ashamed and
disgusted that it happened to me. Why am I talking
about it now? Because that's the wonder of a year in
therapy; I am freeing myself of the humiliation I have
felt, plus the fear of rejection. I don't want to feel those
things any more and they aren't mine to own. I also
work really hard against the type of person who would
question if I am telling the truth, because survivors of
abuse don't owe you any explanation to make you
believe us; we just ask that you respect our bravery for
speaking up. The stark reality of any survivor is they
have been faced with contradiction at least once when
they have spoken up and asked to be heard.

I remember travelling in a car, not too many years
ago really, and talking very openly with a friend about
how angry I felt about having been abused. I said how
much it bothered me, how I was, on the whole, much
more vigilant around my boys because of what had
happened to me, and I was met with disbelief. I was
told it wasn't normal to feel this way and that I needed
help. I was met with disgust. I could feel the disgust
oozing out of their pores, and I went back to being
teen me, who got drunk and would spout out all this
shit and cry because she didn't know how to keep her

emotions in check and would be told to 'just stop talking about it'. I felt like a freak, I felt the shame, and it only further reinforced this idea that I should keep my fucking mouth shut.

What if people judge me? What if people don't believe me? What if I lose people for sharing my truth? What if they think I am now an abuser because I've been abused?

These thoughts might not make sense to other people, but they have been the belief system I've lived by, the reasons I've told myself as to why I should never speak up. I have felt so ashamed, like somehow it was my fault. I wish I was someone else sometimes; maybe someone braver than me, or more successful even. Like, if I could remove myself from the body of someone abused, I could reach my full potential rather than living with this gut-churning idea of myself.

For all those times men inappropriately touched me on a night out and I lost my shit over it, which then led to them telling me to calm down because it was 'just a joke' and me feeling like I was the one who'd overreacted, that maybe I was the one with the problem . . . it was all shame. Other girls liked that attention, so why didn't I? What was wrong with me?? Speaking up was so unbelievably painful that over time I just became more and more silent about my struggles and felt like all I could do was amplify the voices of other people's misjustices.

That sounds heroic but it isn't, because it is only continuing to be part of the problem of not speaking up and having your voice heard. Shame is there from the moment we are born; it is fed to us from the moment we are able to hear voices and see people because it all comes down to the actions of those around us, and what they speak up for. We can all be raised in the most grounded, stable home but that doesn't mean outside influences won't change how we grow.

I don't like to be touched by other men; this is my body and I own it. That is okay. It is alright that I use my voice to say STOP! No one else owns me; I'm not a fucking Fiat Punto with her hazard lights on, attracting attention. I am a woman who should be allowed to feel safe in my own body, regardless of what that might mean to someone else. They aren't me and I am not them. Respecting that decision is acknowledging the importance to them and, actually, I believe helps that person to feel more empowered and less ashamed.

I am talking about shame like it only exists for women who are inappropriately touched, or abused, but really it's just one big issue that I have found in my life.

In the early part of 2021, when I was so desperate for help, calling my doctor's surgery constantly, desperate for something to make everything better, I was clearly taking up a lot of NHS time, and I felt like a massive burden on everyone. My family, the school my children went to, the NHS – everyone. I apologised to the doctor I was talking to down the phone. I was met with a long, painful silence. They said nothing: they didn't want to soothe my hurt or reassure my panic. I felt heartbroken at the time; I needed them to say it was okay, I needed them to tell me not to be ashamed for getting help. They didn't and I have learned from that experience that no matter where you are, who you are with, and what situation you are faced with, you do deserve respect. You don't deserve to feel ashamed of who you are. I never want to allow someone that level of control over me again. To have the power to make me believe my feelings are something to be embarrassed about, to be ashamed of.

I have always wondered: would I have been different if I hadn't been abused? All round I would have definitely been less fucking mental, but I mean, would I have been a little more carefree in my teen years? Would I have worried less about the shame of sleeping around and getting a name for myself? Would I have

41

been less scared of men? I don't know how to answer these questions. How can I? It's impossible to even begin to imagine because this is sadly the life I've had and no amount of regret or sadness can take away from the fact I didn't get a choice over the horrible things that happened to me.

I wanted the college slutty years, I wanted the blow job in the park or the tit wank in a mate's car. I just wanted to be part of something I felt like I was missing; I was yearning to not care! To let go of my shame around how I thought my body looked, and of my inability to know what I was meant to be doing with it. I was toned and tiny – I truly had the most beautiful body, and yet it just didn't look like what I had seen across magazines and in movies. My bikini line, even at 16, was well outside my knicker line and I just didn't know what the fuck to do with it!! SHIT, how could I even think about going to get waxed when I was way too humiliated to show my body to make a change to it? So, when it came to boys, it felt like the easiest thing to do was flirt and then stop before it got any further because I was just frozen with the fear of what my body looked like bare and bold to anyone else.

That is the power of rejection, shame and just not fitting in. I was a teenage girl when someone took the piss out of the fact I had pubes. I was mortified. *I HAVE PUBES . . . AAGGGHHHHH!! That most definitely means no one else has them so I AM FUCK-ING DOOMED.* How was I supposed to know they were a completely normal thing for a girl my age to have? Why, all of a sudden, was my female body something to be ashamed of? This is the shame game we play, and it goes back even further than those early years when the worst thing about your life was the fact you'd fucking grown pubic hair.

We are shamed for everything!

We can be shamed for what we wear – 'That looks too tight on you.'

We can be shamed for how much we eat – 'Are you sure you need another serving of that?'

We can be shamed for how we feel – 'Why would you think that? That is so weird.'

We can be shamed for who we choose to be with – 'Are you sure they're right for you? We don't like them.'

We can be shamed for how we live – 'Wow, your house is a bit of a mess.'

We can be shamed for our children – 'Your kids are a bit mental.'

None of those things are too far-fetched for anyone to imagine happening. I know I can say I have heard each of the above at least once in my life and they all lead to feeling a level of resentment that we haven't managed to do something right. We aren't living up to someone else's expectations. I find it so fucking exhausting and INFURIATING that I let these stupid fucking comments impact me!! I don't want to give a shit about what someone else says about how I run my home, or how my kids behave, and I don't want someone to tell me how I am managing my fucking diet either.

I have felt in the very pit of my stomach a level of revulsion for myself, and it can come on so suddenly, the unconscious trigger being activated and letting loose across my whole body something that makes me feel disgusted by myself. I hate that feeling; it makes me so sad I could cry now because whenever I describe it, I can feel it there, like it's just hanging out at a bar waiting to pounce on me like some unsuspecting victim.

We are all victims and survivors of shame. Don't you think? I mean, it's not like it's a wonderful feeling to have, that makes us go all weak in the knees. For me, it's a physical feeling that, when it comes over me, isn't a nice experience. So does that not make us all victims of how it makes us feel? Or more survivors, I guess, because I prefer that word; it feels more empowering.

Why have I personally felt shame on such a huge level? The trauma I have previously experienced is a massive contributing factor. We all feel shame but, for some of us, the depths it goes are on another level. I can, for instance, tell you about something I did four years ago that I felt ashamed of and how I am a bad person for doing it. I am of this belief that people just don't understand what a terrible person I am. I *know* I'm not a terrible person but as a direct result of emotional trauma, I am – and probably always will be – fighting against the idea that I am truly a disgusting person. I don't even like to type it out, because the truth of it is that it makes me so sad. It is part of the reason why I struggle so painfully with imposter syndrome and don't really understand my own worth.

Shame doesn't go the whole way to explaining why I feel this way, but it is a very large part of it, because as soon as I was properly old enough to understand what had happened to me as a child, and how it wasn't normal for children to live through that, I all of a sudden felt so ashamed it *had* happened to me. Like, it was my fault; that somehow I'd asked for it. I don't like that thought and I like to push it away. I wish I could remove the instant feeling of disgust I get whenever I think about all the times I have fucked up, but I can't.

I am working on it, because above all else I have come to realise I don't deserve to feel this way and actually it isn't a way to live my life. I don't deserve to hate myself on that level, or punish myself for, say, losing my temper five years ago at one of my kids, which instantly made me think at the time that I was an abusive mum.

There is my link: my fear and my shame that I could become the abuser. Because then I would be the worst person on this planet. So, I spend a large proportion of my life trying to convince myself I am doing okay and that I am a good mum. I don't want to write this, like it goes against everything I have ever felt, because you could read this and then think, *Wow!! She is a terrible person.* Then my fears would come true. But I can't avoid how you might think about me because this is who I am and the only thing that has stopped me sharing it is shame. I am ashamed of myself because I hold on to things far more than I would like to admit.

The biggest part about overcoming shame is forgiving yourself; it is without a shadow of a doubt kindness to yourself. It is accepting the fact we are all human and we all carry this heavy agenda of expectation around with us; it's just that some of us carry it a little heavier than others. I have always wanted to be free – to hang up my coat, like I said at the beginning of this chapter – but I realise I'll never escape it, and actually it's not about a game of cat and mouse but more just about forgiving ourselves for all the things we feel we have failed at.

This all feels heavier than my vagina on its period. I don't know how to make this shit fluffy and light. It's hard-hitting and gritty, which wasn't really ever the intention of this book. I like to be entertaining and yet this is the stuff I so desperately want to talk about. Being funny feels easy, but being honest feels harder because we just don't do it; we don't share our shame and we don't like to show it.

I want to offer a light at the end of the tunnel . . . 'YYYAAAYYYY,' I hear you all cry. 'This is wonderful news! She is going to save our lives with a really inspirational list of shit to do to completely rid us of this shitshow!' . . . No, that isn't this list, but here are some things that could and hopefully will help . . .

Write a list of things you are grateful for:
- My husband
- My children
- Cadbury
- *Keeping Up with the Kardashians*

- Laughing
- My bed
- The sun
- Bumblebees (who doesn't love a bee???)

Just brainstorm it; get it out on paper. There is no order of favourites unless you really want to do it that way. Throw it all down and look at it. You don't have to own it. It doesn't need to be big or grand but it needs to be things you are really grateful for. I have even written 'my fridge' before, and 'the radiators in my house'. Making that list of things is powerful in showing you the things that are worthy of your positive focus rather than your negative energy.

Acknowledge it – the thing you feel ashamed about. While the biggest thing I would say to you is that you make sure you do this safely and not tackle potential trauma head-on without the help and guidance of a professional, I am also asking you to see if there is a way of just acknowledging: *This happened and actually when I think about it I feel vile for it, but was it really my fault? Am I really a bad person? Did I learn from it?* Because the most important thing we can do when making mistakes in life is to learn from them.

Forgive yourself. No one should ever make you feel like you need to forgive someone else who hurt you, mistreated you or did something so utterly shit that it changed the course of your life. No one should force that level of forgiveness on you. But I would urge you – I beg of you – to actually learn how to forgive *yourself.* Part of that process sometimes is just acknowledging that you are being hard on yourself and that you make yourself a promise to maybe be a little kinder in how you speak to yourself. You aren't meant to nail this on day one, it's a journey, so stick with it; that goes for allowing people in and out of our lives. It too is a journey of understanding that you deserve more, and that the shitty things people have done to you in the past don't represent the kind of person *you* are, they represent them.

Positive self-chat replaces the negative. Every time you're about to tell yourself you aren't enough – that you are a failure, a bitch, unworthy – replace it with something soothing. Replace it with the thing you would say to your kid when they fall over. No, not 'Don't fucking start crying and get the fuck up off the floor'; instead let it be the really nurturing part of you that says, 'I'm so sorry you're hurt, but actually I think you are really brave.' For me it started with just gently reflecting on the fact I deserved to be nicer to me. It started with whenever I said anything negative about myself, I felt that comment but worked on finding a good thing about me. It felt overwhelming to start because it turned out I said nothing nice about myself, but I then realised it's okay because I have time. I can learn to find a little more space inside of me to love me.

Positive affirmations. These have had a profound effect on my recovery from my mental health issues in recent months. I wish I had realised sooner how powerful they are. I wish I had actually acknowledged the fact that starting every day with a positive quote about how strong I am could have such a lasting impact.

Tell the inner bully to have a night off. I mean, they'll come back after a few minutes with an opening line of 'And another thing . . .' but you just need to remind that part of your brain that you have control for now and they can go chill out for a while. They don't need to be on duty all the time; they can fuck off from time to time too, but you need to tell them that.

Learn from the thing you regret and just try to take another approach the next time. If you fuck it up that time too, it's okay to forgive yourself and start again. This whole 'we must get it right all the time' malarkey must have been created by someone who wasn't human because I will be fucked if this magically godlike being exists, who makes the wisest of decisions, never gets angry and is always above it all. If they do, I don't want to meet them; I already feel pissed off by the idea of them.

Shame is instilled in us by the people we surround ourselves with, how they speak to us, what we absorb from the world and what we have endured. We need to feel a little prouder of where we have come from and where we are going. We need to accept the fact that we can't completely remove shame from who we are – the issue is an impossible thing to tackle – but how we choose to personally address it is where the power will always lie.

I wish I could go back and relive all the moments where I have allowed shame to overshadow any success I've ever had. I wish I could have silenced the voice in my head the day my first book came out that told me I wasn't good enough to be published. I couldn't enjoy what should have been an exceptionally proud moment in my life because I was waiting for someone to tell me I had done it wrong, I waited for someone to confirm what I thought: I am shit at what I do. My inner critic was like my biggest enemy; no one could speak to me as negatively as I spoke about myself.

I have always loved writing and often made up stories, but I enjoy getting what goes on inside my head down onto paper. To those of you reading this and thinking, *Why is she only talking about women's shame?* let me say this: this book isn't for everyone, and I stand by that conviction. I can't mould myself to be the person everyone needs; I can only speak of my own personal experience as a woman. I don't want to spend every chapter trying to find balance between how women have often felt but men also feel too because, actually, if that is something you are looking for, you won't find it here. I am okay with that, and if you want that balance, I am not the author to bring it.

I have been crippled with the fear of not encompassing every person and their needs. While I can't cater to that, I also recognise it isn't my responsibility to do that. The responsibility is yours as the reader; you get the power. You have the power to take action over how and what you absorb. You are your responsibility and you have the opportunity to own it. Take your power, enjoy it and revel in the fact; no matter how ugly or heavy it feels, it doesn't need to be the one thing that defines you.

We have the power of our own to decide what we absorb from the outside world and how, but it takes enough self-belief and not too much arrogance to achieve. You see, if you're not too careful you'll just become a bit of a knob who doesn't believe they need to change, and then they stay still in the place they started. Life is going to throw so many curveballs your way, you could end up with whiplash from dodging them. Your shame will show up in different ways and for different reasons but be ready for it. You are in control of how you feel about yourself and you have the right to rebut the fuck out of what someone does or how they make you feel. We don't have to solely rely on someone else's opinion of us to know we are worthy of more than the shitty things we might think about ourselves. Shame doesn't come with many positives. In fact, the more I think about it the less I can see any!! We just have to know it is within all of us and it'll show up in different ways. The more you get to know how and why shame ticks, the more you begin to see it in how people behave, especially if they feel threatened or embarrassed.

So, fuck shame and all it comes with. No, we can't outrun it and we most definitely won't manage a carefree life without it, but we can live with it knowing it's not just our problem. It is basically our fucking crazy great-great-great-great-auntie's fault for burning at the stake in a bid to be more sexually liberated . . .

Shame is also kind of in our society no matter if you hide your farts from your husband or you slutdrop a fart into a wastepaper bin in front of him. It isn't a particular-person kind of problem, and so while we might look to the free farter as the person living blissfully free of the things we feel shackled by, the truth is they too are experiencing shame. Just know it's a universal issue that can present itself in so many different ways and is usually because of something that happened at some point in their lives that felt so hard their brains then made them feel so shit about themselves they thought they might shit out their intestines . . . that is basically the scientific response to shame.

FACTS ABOUT SHAME

There are actually very different kinds of shame; it's no straightforward walk in the park. It will very much depend on whatever the fuck is happening in that moment. Obviously the brain doesn't want to make this shit easy for us! It wants to keep us on our toes.

There is the good stuff that kind of comes over you very quickly and leaves you feeling gross about something random. Then there is the type of shame that just makes you feel shit all the time. It's called chronic shame; that's kind of where your self-esteem can really be kicked in the minge. Don't forget your humiliation shame for when people ridicule you for doing something they see as stupid, which then lives on inside you like the haunting of an old house. Or even the shame of when we fuck up, when we don't win at something and feel defeated, like we were never good enough.

All that shit rolled into one makes one hell of a sandwich to bite down on. So, here are some fun facts I've pulled together about shame.

- It is a feeling, not a fact. So, next time you go telling yourself you're a worthless piece of shit, just remember shit belongs in the toilet, not in your head. Flush that thought away and replace it with 'I'm actually doing alright.'

- It makes you question who you are – *What if who I think I am isn't really who I am?* I know you've thought that at least once! YOU ARE AWESOME!
- It has the power to destroy friendships and relationships – the lower you are on the shameometer, the better chance you have to actually have better, stronger, more valuable connections with people. It's simple, really; you attract the good stuff when you pump the good stuff out.
- Everyone feels it – even the people you think are nailing it will have their own shit going on to some degree.
- It feels embarrassing and lonely – no one likes to feel shit about themselves. It feels . . . shameful.
- Shame needs oxygen to breathe, so snuff the fucker out by acknowledging what it looks like.
- People who suffer with heavy shame are more likely to suffer with depression and anxiety. Explains a fucking lot about me, then!

So, those are the facts, but what are we meant to do with them? How can we get a handle on our shame?

- Know that you aren't a bad person – nope. Not even a little bit. I mean, we all have the ability to be a moody cunt from time to time but your mood doesn't make you a bad person. Losing your temper or feeling irritated doesn't make you an arsehole.
- Take a little risk in life – go on, tell the mate you've got piles . . . or maybe just start with walking around the house naked first.
- Think of all the witches that died in the quest of an orgasm. They tried to release the shame shackled to women for believing they deserved more. WE DESERVE MORE and even they saw it back then.
- Don't blame yourself for everything – you can't control life and you most definitely aren't to blame for all the bad stuff that happens.
- Don't suppress it – let those feelings out into the wide world, no matter how weird they feel. The more you try to avoid it, the harder the shame game plays.
- Don't make your shame someone else's – you don't need to make someone else feel shit

because you feel shit. We are all responsible for ourselves and so that also means sometimes you are going to need to hold yourself accountable for the way you behave.

But even with the knowledge of what to do when you feel it, you may still be asking yourself, *How do I know if what I'm feeling is shame?*

I have talked about the below already but it is really important to note more examples here now because the list of physical feelings around shame is huge. You would be hard pushed to find anyone who could tick off every single symptom of shame, which I think is why at times it can be quite hard to pinpoint when you're feeling shame unless you get the deeper meaning behind why you're feeling it.

Here are just some of the signs of shame:

- Feeling super-sensitive – not just 'first day of your period' kind of sensitive either.
- Feeling like everyone takes advantage of you.
- Feeling afraid of looking stupid.
- Perfectionism.
- Low self-esteem.
- Not wanting to be the centre of attention.
- Trust issues.

- Being the social chameleon.
- Feeling as if you have no identity.
- Needing to have the last word.
- Paranoia.
- Fear of failure.

To be honest, the list is really extensive because shame is basically the ick feeling you get about anything in your life where you feel repulsed by yourself, you feel defensive over who you are, you regret what you do. I mean, it's fucking big.

See, fixing something like shame is hard because we are all living a life with those things to a certain extent, so understanding and seeing how we behave is hard because those things all really heavily link into poor self-esteem, surrounding yourself with shit people and believing you aren't worthy of more.

People who suffer with shame on a big scale – like the 'if it was an Olympic sport they'd win gold' kind of level – are often those who are survivors of childhood trauma, who've been the victim of bullying, who never feel like their emotions are met, who have been rejected or have suffered mental and physical abuse.

Remember, shame is a normal response; it's how we kind of navigate life in some ways because it's figuring out what to do and not do based on our social surroundings. But shame can also feel heavier than my arse sat on someone's face. It can be really all-consuming and it does destroy people's lives. It isn't a fun thing to experience but it's really important to know how to soothe ourselves when it hits.

I want to soothe my own icks but I also know sometimes that isn't always going to be possible because it'll really depend on my mood, where my period is and how my mental health is feeling. My hope for this side chapter is just that it helps you realise you aren't alone in feeling shame and to help you see how it can really manifest in so many areas of our lives. I have rejected tackling things I have felt shame over in the past based purely on the fact they felt too heavy to deal with. I didn't want to feel them, but accepting them just felt way too much, so I just tried to ignore them in the hope they would go away. I mean, make sense of that one?!

You're not alone in your shame, but more importantly you can heal from it. Not entirely, but it doesn't have to rule your life and make you feel like you are stuck within the prison walls it has built for you. You can break free, but that takes time and self-love.

CHAPTER 3

Boundaries

Where do I start? How can I even bring you the answers to boundaries when I am still learning my own? I think I'll start with breaking down what they look like and why they are important while also reading back what I say to myself and repeating the saying: my boundaries are important! Without these essential boundaries I would have struggled so much more with my recovery. They are part of the tools I have learned to live by to keep myself safe and grounded.

Such a fun word. BOUNDARIES. *Your* boundaries. These little fuckers can be a total bitch to set, because they are yours. They don't look like everyone else's. You have to keep reinforcing them for yourself but also for the people around you. You have to keep reminding them, because these boundaries aren't someone else's responsibility. They are yours, and yours alone.

You just have to hope that the people around you will respect them and try to nurture them for you. It's important for any healthy relationship to thrive that these people – whether they are your parents, your partner or your friend – understand why they are so fucking sacred and that is purely because anyone who does truly want what's best for you will support your happiness.

Yes, during this process you are going to lose people; you could call it a natural weeding-out process. They might not like the different version of you who decides what she wants or even who she needs to be around, but you will learn there are people you need to let go of in order to protect yourself. That is okay! I've realised my life goal now is to hear the words 'Wow, you've changed' and for me to not take it as an insult but as more of a compliment, whether the person meant it in an arsehole way or not. I *have* changed and, shit, it feels good to be here, thank you very much!

FYI: the fact that you will lose people along the way is another thing that makes boundaries fucking hard to keep. Why? Because you already have a broom shoved up your arse sweeping the floor, and you also now need to constantly set your own fucking emotional parameters for other people who are too stupid to remember them.

I hear you, but actually the reality is that, without them, we only ever learn to please other people. I am a semi-professional trying hard not to make it to the big leagues of people-pleasing. It can look a lot like this:

- 'Yes, I'll come' (*I don't want to go*).
- 'Of course I will help' (*I really don't want to help*).
- Smiling for everyone else (crying on the inside).
- Saying sorry for everything (even breathing at the wrong time).
- Being a social chameleon to fit into your surroundings: 'Yes, oh, I agree, absolutely!' (*Actually I think you are full of shit but I absolutely can't disagree with you because then you won't be my friend.*)
- Feeling good about yourself because that person over there liked what you said (but this time tomorrow you'll feel shit again because someone didn't say something nice to you).

Is that you? It is, isn't it? The people-pleaser . . . she loves to maintain the idea that making everyone else happy, being an empath – and putting her own needs so far down the pecking order they're not even on the same page – is the right way to live life. Well, I am here to tell you all those things you/we do will always successfully maintain the ideas, wants and needs of everyone around you . . . except YOU.

Just hear me out, I want to pop this idea into your head. You can say no. Don't start replying in your head with a 'but' – just swim with the idea of saying no to something you don't want to do. Even if it's the washing. Go on: say no. Now ask why. Why do you want to say no? Do you feel burned out? Exhausted? Sad? What is it that's stopping you from wanting to do that thing or be around that person? Just stop to think: what is popping up in your head over and over? I actually can't answer that for you, but you can. What is it? There will be a different answer for each thing you want to resist. Often the answer lurking like a stalker in the night is that thing you need to change. Change is healthy, if it is in your best interest.

Most often, my reason for not wanting to do something is rooted in my fears of abandonment and conflict. Abandonment goes all the way back to my childhood, when I felt threatened by my abuser that, if I spoke up and told anyone what was happening to me, my whole family would leave me. Obviously that wasn't true, but when you're that young, completely overpowered and totally at the mercy of someone else, that shit sinks in. It has taken me going through therapy to realise that the level of fear I have that someone will leave me if I say what I want is because I am, above all else, trying to protect myself from unwanted hurt or pain. My brain tells me the easiest way to do this is to make others happy, and ignore what I want or need.

As for the conflict, does anyone really love it? The drama? All the shit that goes with kicking off every single time you do something that goes against the grain? I think if you love and enjoy the attraction of that level of shit in your life it does beg the question, why? I personally don't, but I am the first person to defend someone else. I will fiercely rip the throat out of anyone who dares to hurt my children (obviously not literally), or anyone I love. I am so protective of them but not of myself.

I have, in many respects, continued to allow people to control me into doing what they want, because I just want to fit into life where I don't massively fit in anyway. I just want to feel the acceptance of that person, even though that feeling they give back will always be fleeting. I have always liked the feeling of being praised. I think that is pretty normal but I came to realise I was actually almost solely relying on someone else's ideas of me, what they thought I was and why I should have been proud or ashamed. I worked on the basis that if it made them happy, it must be the right thing to do. I idolised people to the extent that everything that came out of their mouth would be gospel and I would think I had to change to fit into their ideas because they just had the key to life. They knew it all!! I have since realised literally no one has that – no one. It isn't normal to have everything figured out. It isn't healthy to just take on situations with literally no emotion and pretend like nothing hurts. It is not okay to live up to the expectations of someone else's ideas.

I have been working really hard this year at saying the following:

'No, thank you.'

Not because having boundaries makes you a hostile bitch, but because it is giving me the power back. People don't have to like the words, they don't have to understand, but they do need to learn to respect them. Whether they like it or not, if they truly love you they will learn to understand you are putting yourself first, which is the most important thing you could ever do.

You will no doubt lose people. When you are a people-pleaser, you can often attract people in your life who understand that, because you never say no, they can take the piss.

Your boundaries, your priority, your mantra – you don't have to do what other people say to make them happy.

Being a people-pleaser doesn't mean you have some kind of past with sexual abuse, like I have; it is a natural way to protect yourself. Remember that. Your brain doesn't want to hurt you; it is fundamentally screwed by thinking the best way to protect you is to make sure you serve other people and their needs. It will no doubt remember a time when you put yourself first and felt pain, rejection or conflict for doing that, so it learned that you needed to adapt to survive. 'Survive' sounds very extreme, like you're living in the Amazon jungle and you need to protect yourself from a man-eating cobra. The most wonderful thing about our brain is it will try its best to keep you from harm. It just doesn't always know the best course of action. This is fine, because all we need to do is teach it how to take baby steps away from the things it thinks are working for you.

It doesn't have to be some really powerful, grand reveal of the NEW YOU, and fuck everyone else. It just has to be small, manageable steps you can take and maintain. It's like deciding you're going to run a marathon when you've never run before; you don't just step outside the house and run 26 miles. It takes time, and the only way you will actually manage to complete that marathon is if you actually slowly maintain your progress. No need to be like a bull in a china shop, and within a week have gone back on 19 of the 20 new things you introduced. This is the long run, hunny, so pace yourself. Give yourself the time and energy it is going to take to stay in it for the long run.

Another thing we have to learn alongside setting boundaries is how to stop saying sorry all the time. 'I am sorry I punched you in the face', 'I am sorry I stabbed you with that knife' or 'I am sorry I deliberately farted on you' are all necessary apologies; they have true meaning and they are (hopefully) genuine. 'I am sorry I was in your way', 'I am sorry my chair touched your chair', 'I am sorry I was looking at you', 'I am sorry I didn't put my make-up on', 'I am sorry I haven't made dinner yet' are, however, completely not required. Nope, not one of them.

Saying sorry for everything actually devalues the word and meaning, and yet here I am saying the same fucking 'I am sorry' words over and over. For what, Laura? STOP SAYING SORRY because you're only doing it to fit in and to make people like you, or trust you, or believe you. Like, if you cower at their knees and ask for forgiveness over something so min-ute that they didn't even notice, then maybe they'll accept you. Even if you don't want to be accepted by them, you'll still try your fucking best to do it because weirdly you still need their nod of approval that it's okay. I would like to officially tell you all I am trying my best to work on saying sorry less and understand-ing the fact this word should be reserved for times when I actually really need to say it. I don't need to be ashamed of all the times I've messed up and had to apologise; everyone makes mistakes and they are all repairable – unless you murder someone and then that is pretty much not alright.

Sometimes stepping back and addressing what you really need is the most empowering thing you could ever do. It isn't easy; if it was easy everyone would be so secure in themselves that the pages of this book would be fucking useless. Remember that the brain is designed to make you survive so it'll often go around in the same old boring loop of: I can't change because this will happen, or that will happen. You are entitled, though. Stepping away from someone that doesn't necessarily help your mental health or support the emotional needs you have isn't a walk in the park. It actually takes a lot of strength.

Our boundaries are really important, and actually they are perfectly acceptable. If meeting that friend makes you feel like you're about to spew that chicken wrap from lunch back up then why the fuck are you going? To please them? No, babes, this isn't the right way around. The mood hoover in your life doesn't have to be there just because you feel a sense of loyalty, and it's going to take some processing, understanding and time to figure out how to remove yourself with the least amount of trauma possible, but do it, because you deserve positive relationships with people. Walking away from someone else's plane crash feels alarming if you have a good heart because you don't want to hurt others, but where is your oxygen mask?? If it's 50 miles away and meanwhile you're on a plane over the Bahamas, how are you ever expected to survive this person's catastrophe without it then becoming yours to own too?? In that I mean, this plane isn't your responsibility so when their wreck happens, do not fall into the wreckage with it. The process of elimination in your life comes down to how much you need that person, for their good, bad and ugly. You don't have to be responsible for their happiness, but you do have to be responsible for your own.

This might look like taking a step back; regardless of what shit might be happening in their life, the most important, precious thing you have right now is you. Maybe it looks like taking a walk alone away from your partner, maybe it looks like saying no to that friend who is desperate to meet you, maybe it's standing down as the person responsible for your kid's school disco. The world isn't relying on your sole input, and it will continue to spin if you take a minute to catch your breath.

One of the most precious skills you can learn is how to comfort yourself. I don't mean putting on a nice pair of joggers with your slippers; I mean finding what brings you the most comfort in your inner self. What brings you the most control in your life? Knowing how to keep yourself in check further strengthens you to keep the boundaries that make you feel safe, and to stay in control of your own life.

I am not saying I have my boundaries nailed. I had always hoped they would appear in my mind like a little bullet-point check list when faced with a decision over something. Life moves way too fast for that to happen and sometimes we are going to need to say yes to things we don't want to do: going for the smear test, seeing the dentist, going to therapy. None of those things have us high-fiving the air because it'll be so much fun, and we can easily find ways to avoid these things, but actually they are part of our essential care. There is a difference between choosing to say no to something that could impact someone else's mood, and saying no to something that is basically there to keep you safe or healthy.

I spent the vast majority of 2021 proving to myself why I could do the little things I had completely taken for granted. I could leave the house, I could even turn my phone's WhatsApp notifications back on. I could make my children dinner. Granted, none of those things feel like a personal boundary, but it was more that I had literally had everything taken from me. I had nothing, so finding my own boundaries meant I had to build everything back up to figure out what I needed to get rid of and make room for the other things that were more important or valuable to me.

I had to end relationships that didn't make me happy and it was important I did it with my interests at heart. I didn't want to hurt anyone; my intention is to never harm someone else, but unfortunately, in the process of doing something someone doesn't like,

I will hurt them. They will no doubt go on to hate me, and while my knee-jerk reaction to that is to say sorry, I HAVE TO resist the feeling of apologising because I can't say sorry any more for choosing myself over someone else. I can't feel bad for losing something that in the long run actually hurt me emotionally.

I can assure you I didn't nail those relationship exits either – I was like an awkward teen trying to end it with his girlfriend over WhatsApp – but I forgive myself for all the shortcomings I might have had over what I might not have done perfectly because I am human and I did ultimately protect myself, which I am, in turn, really proud of myself for.

I didn't just wake up one day and say: well, today is the day I change everything and I put all my wonderful walls up covered in roses to protect me. It just doesn't happen like that, but it is about taking more time to pause and acknowledge how to feel when responding to something in life. We do have choice and it's important to remember that choice is ours.

Although I mentioned the essential care of medical appointments, it is also important your boundaries are met there too. If you don't like a certain doctor, fucking well say it. They might have a fantastic qualification, but that doesn't mean they know how to treat YOU individually and all your needs. A personal boundary of mine is that I struggle to have male medical professionals examine me. Have I in the past not said this because I don't feel I am entitled to that level of care? Yes. Is that okay? No! It is actually devastating. I remember being 17 and finding a lump in my breast. I made an appointment and asked to see a female doctor. A male came in; I again asked for a female. He left. Came back and said there was no one else around. A female was present while he did the exam, but was this okay? No! Why? Because it made me feel uncomfortable, for good reason. Even if I didn't have good reason, my boundaries were crossed, and I have since then been faced with many situations where I've not wanted a man present but that's happened anyway. I have never felt it appropriate to say, 'I am a survivor of sexual abuse and I don't want a man.' I didn't know how to form those words. I had learned that it was something I had to silently carry because it didn't feel like it should be a good enough reason to demand a female doctor.

What do boundaries look like in a simple way? Putting yourself first. Even before your kids, which I know feels a completely alien thought because it's not what we are designed to do. However, in actual fact we become better people when we make sure our wants and needs are met. I don't mean a four-week cruise around the Med because that obviously isn't quite as achievable, but giving yourself the opportunity to declutter your mind is actually healthy. Giving yourself the time to work out what you want from life is perfectly acceptable. You don't have to just be the yes girl all your life; there is stepping outside of your comfort zone for *you*, and then there is doing it for everyone else.

If you ask the question – what do I WANT? And the answer that comes back is 'I just don't know', that is okay; it's gonna be okay. You don't have to know. I wish it were that easy, but it just isn't – I cannot tell you how much my toes have curled as I have made decisions based on what I need. It has gone against everything I have ever known, but I think what I have realised while making these decisions is I do deserve them. While I deserve them, I am also having to learn about them, so when you are faced with the inner panic of 'I don't know the answer for me!!' just remember: you are a work in progress. It will come in time once you allow yourself to truly figure out what it is you would like. It is also okay to sometimes answer with, 'I don't know. Can I get back to you?' Why do you have to give a yes or no answer?? You don't, and people have to learn patience. You could probably do with giving yourself a smidge of that patience too.

There could be people who read this chapter and think, *What a piece of piss!* Having to find yourself and just saying no when you don't want to do something. It all sounds so easy, so straightforward. However, unless you have learned through your trauma responses to never trust yourself and to leave your life decisions down to someone else, I don't think you can begin to imagine how hard it is to make choices based on your own thoughts and needs. I didn't realise how much of a people-pleaser I was until I fully admitted to myself that's what I had been doing, because I would have a million excuses rather than facing the truth of it. I am too scared to trust myself, I don't know how to do it. I haven't been taught, and I haven't learned how to.

I completely relied upon everyone else to tell me how I felt. If I felt sad I would ask Steve to tell me how I should be feeling. He met that need – he would reassure me with a softer version of what I might be feeling – and yet actually that need would soon need meeting again and, instead of trusting myself, my own decisions and my own feelings, I would once again reach out to him. By the time I had my breakdown in January 2021, I was relying on him sometimes hourly to tell me the same thing: 'Everything is going to be okay; you are going to get through this; you are strong enough.'

It was as exhausting as it sounds. All I needed to do was trust my own feelings, go with whatever they were telling me, and start on my boundaries of where I needed to be to have more safety and control in my life, and yet I absolutely didn't. I was at the mercy of yet another man and his thought process over what I should be doing. As toxic and unhealthy as that relationship was, I was using Steve to be the more dominant person in my life, to call the shots (even though the bastard can't even decide what to eat for dinner most nights) and make the decisions. It wasn't through any fault of Steve; thank God he was as patient and kind as he was because he just constantly reassured my recovery and looked at things far more rationally than I could at that time.

I wasn't actually respecting any of his boundaries and I was just sapping the fucking life out of him. He was completely unable to set any personal boundaries either. So, this really unhealthy co-dependency continued – mainly my dependence on him but also, on his side, his unwavering fear of leaving me because I might do something dangerous. It has taken both of us to acknowledge that and do something about it to even start to heal the

wounds. We have had to have some really painful conversations where we have openly talked about what
hasn't been helpful and what we would like to change to
maintain any form of marriage. I honestly think if we
hadn't had those conversations, we probably would have
eventually ended up separating.

You can see how people repeat the same cycles of
unhealthy behaviours, because they aren't breaking the
loop. They aren't challenging the thought process.
They aren't dedicating time to work on themselves,
and instead fall back into toxic relationships, and make
mentally dangerous decisions basically because they
haven't learned the difference between making a
healthy choice based on what they NEED rather than
what they are used to.

This is coming from a person who has a pretty
wholesome relationship with her husband – he is my
best friend, he is my soul mate – and yet we've had to
have conversations about the unhealthy attachments
we have formed with each other. We met really young,
we both yearned for someone, we basically both
wanted loads of sex, but we were both victims of
trauma from our own childhoods for different reasons,
and so we kind of clung to each other, not really knowing how to exist without one another. We have wanted

some form of stability we hadn't tried to find in ourselves because we never learned how to be in a healthy relationship and also maintain our own mental health.

I am happy to say, these are all things we are working on because we love each other enough and want to continue to grow in finding our own feet. Neither of us can be sure about where that'll take us or where it'll end. Who knows, it could end in our marriage being over – and while I can only hope that won't happen, I don't think I could ever be that smug to say life is just one straightforward line, because people change. I have seen first-hand this last year how fast stuff changes and how much of yourself can feel and look different. It could be that the more we set our own boundaries, the more we don't recognise each other any more. I have said on more than one occasion to him in these last 18 months, with tears clinging to my cheeks, that I don't care what happens as long as we're both happy.

I have come away from that time in my life desperate to never, ever rely on someone else like that again. Maybe that's what kick-started my need for boundaries? Maybe it's because everything I googled talked about healthy boundaries and where to find them. I don't know, but I do know I have never felt more out of control over my life than the time I completely relied upon my husband to rule it, even though he did it begrudgingly and wished to have his wife back who wasn't so scared of every decision she was faced with, down to setting her own bedtime.

So, how did I do it? Slowly. I tried to slow down and figure out what I wanted.

Day one: I would like to invite myself to get out of bed.

Day two: I would like to invite myself to wear something I feel good in.

Day three: I would like to invite myself to get out of bed (sometimes the thing about this is we are having to reinforce those little boundaries to make room for the new ones) and I would like to put the TV on.

Day four: I would like to invite myself to go out into the back garden.

. . .

Week six: I would like to invite myself to go to the shop and focus on what I am looking to buy and not how I think people might be looking at me. I don't need to focus on smiling at anyone, making conversation or being polite.

. . .

Week twelve: I would like to invite myself to bravely type out that message wishing someone well and delicately telling them I need space in my life to find more happiness.

When you start working on putting in boundaries in your life, you need to start with the small stuff and work up to the bigger stuff. It is about working out what you need, what brings you happiness or safety, before you can figure out the next part. If that is putting on the TV, then fucking start there!

You see, you don't just DO IT! You work at it. You spend time living in it, in the moment. Setting boundaries isn't this massive grand statement of dedication to a life you HAVE to live. Boundaries are kinder than that; they are more forgiving and less aggressive. They don't need to be huge and unmaintainable. Above all else, they are there to gently love you a little more and nurture you a little harder. They aren't your enemy. They aren't there to destroy you and everything around you. They are there to keep you living for you and not everyone else. The moment you surrender to the idea you were put here on this planet for you is the moment you can truly start living.

I know that sounds like some really cheesy one-liner that you get inside a fortune cookie (maybe that's where I got it from) but it's true. I have never felt more alone and desperate than when I was left with nothing because I had spent a whole life completely resisting and ignoring the idea of living how I wanted to live. I did all the cookie-cutter stuff: I married my teen sweetheart, I had the mortgage, the kids and the life, and yet I still fell really fucking hard. I have had the most unhealthy boundaries with people around me, including my husband, and probably indirectly my children, all because I lacked any idea of how powerful it is to just work on accepting and offering myself to the world as the person who makes her own decisions for herself.

Boundaries shouldn't ever be set in stone; they should flow like a river running alongside your life and they should always have your best interests at heart. No one can tell you what they should look like or how they should feel because sadly, given the opportunity, we are invariably going to want to shape that person's boundaries to suit our needs. So, when someone is pushing against the things you feel are important, wholesome or even healthy for you, push back! You don't need to keep finding reasons to move your goal posts while they take up more of the playing field; this isn't their life! It is yours, and, regardless of who they are, they will never be entitled to make those calls.

I've had to have conversations where I've had to diplomatically shut down things I just don't want to talk about or delve into. I have had to ask people to not tell me certain things because I've known they would in turn piss me off! I will feel a need to retaliate or feel hurt and offended and I have come to realise that sometimes you just don't need to hear it and the most powerful thing you can do is to shut it the fuck down. There could be a part of you desperate to hear what they might want to say, to then come back with a response, but for who? Why? Where do you benefit? I think it's about the forfeit of life. You sometimes have to call it and realise you are a better person for not reading it, listening to it or arguing it. It has been heartbreaking as someone who hasn't found that second nature because I have been desperate for someone to just say, 'You did the right thing,' but I just try really hard now to tell myself I did the right thing for me. I avoided the drama to maintain my nervous system, I shut the conversation down to protect my heart and I stepped back to remind everyone, including myself, why my boundaries are so fucking important.

That whole notion of 'what other people say about you is none of your business' kind of fits with the idea of boundaries. Sometimes the things people say about us hurt, and it's so good and nourishing to be reminded that we do not deserve to feel bad about ourselves based on someone else's limited view or opinion of us. Allow yourself the space and tranquillity of finding yourself and what is important to you.

There is this saying of 'you do you', which is great, but until you know what the *you* looks like and feels like, that can be really overwhelming to try to tackle. Find the people who will help you on this journey, the people who won't judge, who don't demand and who'll understand.

CHAPTER 4

Pussy Posse

Where is my pussy POOOSSEEEEEEE?? Come grab life by the vagina with me and let's find our way together, collectively propping up ourselves and each other through the process. Why can't we own the world? Have anything we ever dreamed of together? Oh, that's right, because we don't live in Narnia! (Although the queen in Narnia was a bit of an egocentric prick herself, so that might be a poor example to start with.)

We aren't very good at sharing and holding space for other women. We believe if we give that space to another woman, we are going to ultimately run out of breathing room.

Men, generally speaking, are paid more, have more liberation to move as they please and can chase dreams. Women who chase dreams beyond settling down and having children are often demonised. It's true! We don't like women who succeed in life; it feels threatening.

I think it is threatening for men because it damages their precious egos that a woman could potentially do something better than them. It is also damaging to women because we feel inferior for not managing to succeed at something we could have done but instead we chose not to chase the dream.

I know that sounds harsh and yet, even down to the reality shows we see splashed across Netflix or Amazon Prime (like *Keeping Up with the Kardashians*, where they constantly fucking fight with each other, or the Real Housewives of whatever given fucking city – my guilty pleasure, by the way), you see the woman who believes in herself as the enemy – the one who shows fewer insecurities, and behaves like an ego-driven man, to be the bitch. We don't like women to be successful and, because it is so much harder for women to achieve success, they often feel the need to behave a certain way to get there – AKA the bitch who steps on all other women to get to the top.

I have had nowhere near as many conversations with men who said their ultimate dream in life was to become a dad as I've had with women, who I've heard talk openly about how becoming a mother felt like their birthright. But that maternal desire ends up working against us – being a mum is seen as our limitation. Meanwhile, men who have a family at home aren't seen as being held back by their personal responsibilities; in fact, they probably even get put up for promotions just based on some old-fashioned idea they have a wife and kids to support! But women are generally assumed to be limited in what they can do when they have children to look after, and that in turn can breed contempt among women; when someone moves against something we felt was our womanly limits, we try to cheer them on, but deep down we might feel a smidge bit insecure or jealous.

Like, when a woman does have that career we were taught was suited for men, while maybe balancing a family, we might be screaming inside, *How can you have both??* We have been conditioned to think we should be able to have both while everything around us actively tries to stop us from 'having it all', and I know from personal experience that I have felt inferior compared to those who have managed to chase their dreams while also making a home and life. *Why can't I? What am I doing wrong?*

All of a sudden, this career that someone else chose, a life they managed to carve out for themselves, leaves us asking more questions about who we are, which literally is not their fucking problem. It is ours! Go on, just fucking admit it! I have most definitely felt that level of insecurity because I've seen other women succeed and I've wondered, *What am I doing wrong?!? Where did I take the wrong turn?* All the while chastising myself for all my fuck-ups and overlooking the fact it's perfectly acceptable for me to just cheer the other woman on. It's okay to just be happy for someone who has something you haven't got; it's okay to want to help and support someone in succeeding at what they worked hard for. You don't have to want the same thing as them and you can wish for more than you have, but you need to accept that they deserve it. When your time comes, if you surround yourself with the right kind of people, they too will cheer you on.

We can't expect everyone to have that mentality – they won't – and this book isn't going to change the life of every woman who reads it, so it's more important you find people who just support you.

They don't need to have been in your life forever, they don't need to be family, but they need to be the person or people who brings out the best of you into the world, while you also work on doing that too. Don't forget, it isn't someone else's responsibility to make you shine; you need to know where your light switch is to be brighter than the mother-fucking sun.

You have to love you first before someone else can love you back. No matter how impossibly hard that notion will be to read, it is true. You have to know you are allowed to want more for yourself, and you're allowed to reach for better things. (That bar of Dairy Milk most definitely isn't the best thing going for you right now.) You need to make sure the person you start with is you, which sounds mental because here I am telling you to blow your own trumpet, but I'm saying, have a toot – you are allowed. I think the problem with only ever learning to help others will, in the long run, make you firstly feel like Mother Teresa, who I truly believe had shit days too, but it'll also make you feel resentful when that bird flaps its wings and leaves you behind. Sure, it'll come back to the nest to visit, but if you aren't also learning to fly right along with it, it really does mean you stay where you are and you never explore your true potential.

Your potential is limitless, but you have to believe in yourself to even give it a try.

Have I felt insecure about who I am and whether I belong? ABSOLUTELY. Why? Because I didn't tell myself I belonged there in the first place. Instead I told myself I didn't have it in me to make it, and that everything I had came to me by complete chance, that luck had got me there. I have championed other women, I have gladly celebrated them, but there has always been a part of me that's believed I don't deserve that same level of success. So, being who you are is exceptionally important. Own that person, cherish her, this person – YOU are the most important part about this because you can't begin to shape the person you will be around if you don't work on why you are entitled to have good people in your life who support you. This isn't some in-the-far-distance story for me; it has been as recent as the last year. I have really, really had to focus on what I need in my life and how that supports my overall mental health and happiness.

If you bitch and find fault in everyone, nit-pick their lives, or talk behind their backs, who are you going to surround yourself with? People who are probably likely to do it about you too. We are all capable of change, and I've been this person. I have really recognised that I have bitched about people when I absolutely shouldn't have. I have said nasty shit about things that actually had fuck all to do with me. I have been able to reflect on the fact I did that more often than not because of a deep-down jealousy. Does that make me a massive cunt heading for hell? Potentially, but I can say, hand on my heart, that I am learning to address my jealousy more and the reasons behind why

I feel it – normally because that person's life, success or situation feels better than mine and I hate feeling like I'm a failure.

Repeat after me: THIS IS NOT HEALTHY.

It's okay, just take a moment to accept it. You need to own why you did it. What made you want to be a fucking cowbag about someone's home? Their promotion? Their life? Really, it always comes down to the same thing: We are, deep down, jealous, envious, resentful – call it whatever the fuck you want, but the thing is, how someone else lives their life is not our business or responsibility. It just doesn't have anything to do with us. We don't like to accept the fact we sometimes just have to stand back and clap for them on the way. Whether their success is down to what you feel is luck, or marrying the rich guy, it just isn't our problem to make sense of. Their life, what they've sacrificed or even hidden the truth about, is for them to live with. We all have this bitchbag ugly side and it's okay to admit that. I would actually worry more about your self-inflated opinion of yourself if you didn't have the range of reflection to see that in yourself. No one shits gold bars.

If you can't be that person who claps, then step back. You don't need to be there, and that's alright. That person, as well as you, will be better in the long run if you aren't in each other's lives. If you can't find happiness for that person, that says a lot about the depth of your relationship. In short, there is no fucking depth to it at all.

When I say 'join the pussy posse', that isn't some invitation to invite every Tara, Darcy and Harriette; it's an invitation to form your foundations: the cement, the footings, the stability of your present and future. It's finding the people who help you to build the bricks of your empire. The club can have a specialised guest list only you hand-picked. That doesn't make you a cliquey bitch; it makes you recognise the fact you are entitled to healthy, grounded and nourishing relationships with other women who support your idea of giving and taking in a friendship.

I am trying to listen more to what people are actually saying and judge less for what they might be doing. I need to accept responsibility for the fact I have such a massive role in how other women will continue in life. I am part of so many incredible women's lives and I speak to them sometimes daily, so I need to remember that the way I speak to them can have a massively huge impact. My words and actions have power, and I need to use it wisely – mainly because I need to continue to strive for the things that matter to me, whether that be better mental health or a new car, a new house, an exciting new business venture. I have to want the same level of success for other women too. Being at the top of whatever your game is will be lonely if you don't encourage and help other women on the ride with you.

It's not just one lesson we learn either; it's fluid, it's flexible and it has to change with you. I have probably had some of the most nourishing friendships in my thirties; I have met people who have really spoken to that part of me that made me feel included. I have been able to be ME around those people. I arrive as I am around them. It feels wholesome.

There isn't this finite period of time where you can make your impact. If life worked that way, fashion would have stopped changing decades ago, and technology would be so limited we'd all still be surviving off dial-up. We can rediscover ourselves a million times over if we lean into the idea that we are allowed to and we are capable of it. Changing, building and growing is a gift, but it's gonna take time and, granted, a lot of that time is swallowed up with the niffnaff and bullshit of day-to-day life, which kind of makes life travel at a rate of 100 miles per hour.

Life moves fast, so why waste it on poor friendships and unhappiness? The route to change is through you if you want it.

Do you want to be bitter? I doubt it! Do you want to be angry? I mean, it's a pretty normal human response and yet there are good and healthy reasons as to why we should never stay angry for too long. Do you want to be around people you can't trust? I highly doubt it. I think I have always known this deep down, but I've not really known how to tackle a situation like that. How the fuck do you say, 'Nah, I don't like this space any more; it doesn't bring me happiness any more,' with confidence?

What is stopping you from changing? Fear! Fear of rejection and more than likely of the unknown. Supporting women and ourselves goes hand in hand, and the reason we don't like to do it comes down to a lot of our own insecurities and how we believe we might feel more entitled than someone else.

I've had to make some really big changes in my life this last year or so; I've had to step aside from some friendships I thought I'd have forever and I've had to understand that my pussy posse needs to be hand-picked by the things that are important to me:

- Safety
- Honesty
- Kindness

- Trust
- Love

I also feel it's important to say I like loyalty – and not in a 'whatever I say goes' kind of way, but rather in an 'I can leave the room and feel confident those people aren't talking while I'm gone' way. Why is that important? Because I deserve the work and respect that I put into my relationships. This is my tick list, but what does yours look like?

MAKE A LIST!! Write a list of the things you love about the women in your life. How they empower and encourage others, see strength, build bridges and tenderly carry you with them.

Friendships and girl power will constantly evolve; this is good, it's healthy. Sometimes you will have to let go of women that won't want to be let go of, but remember – you have to put yourself first before you can effectively be the person everyone else wants you to be. This is kind of reinforcing the whole boundaries thing again. Where are your boundaries? Do they matter? They always have, so just remember that. If someone else is getting in the way of you putting yourself first, they need to go. The process of letting them go might not be easy, it might take time, and it might terrify you (it did me) but that's okay. There wasn't some Mexican stand-off where we waited to shoot each other down. I just chose for myself to respectfully give myself space, and find the courage to wish them well, with no hate, and hope that they would just respect my wishes.

It kind of fits into the same realms as stepping out of your comfort zone because, if you are making changes in your life, that person more than likely won't understand and I think it really does just feel safer and more comfortable to stay where you are with less conflict, where things are . . . okay. Not great, but okay. I don't like conflict, it's not something I am drawn to, but because I have avoided it, it's meant I have put up with things I probably shouldn't have and turned a blind eye to comments that maybe hurt or didn't sit right with me. Was that the other person's intention? I will never be able to answer that and actually that's cool with me because I can feel how I feel and not be questioned on whether that is right or wrong. (Hang on a minute . . . what does this sound like??? I know you know! It sounds a lot like BOUNDARIES.)

Sometimes we just have to accept things have run their course and no amount of fitting the old mould you used to fit will make you feel complete. Keep breaking the mould!!

I have found a confidence where I can debate with friends and know it's perfectly healthy. We can share opinions and also respect the other person's point of view. That is called positively being a feminist bad-ass bitch. Being a feminist isn't burning your bra and screaming 'I hate men' into the wind (although often tempting); it is respecting the voice of another woman and encouraging her through whatever she wants to talk about. Whether that be shaving her body hair, or leaving it to grow out like the weeds in my garden.

I'm the weed-growing garden hair grower. (Bear with me, guys, I feel a rant about body hair coming on . . .) And I am kind of in two minds over where I stand with it, because I DO shave my armpits and feel nothing but complete rage and resentment that men don't have to – because, to be honest, it just looks fucking cool on them and sexy – whereas women are outwardly shamed for any suggestion of body hair. I remember Julia Roberts going to a film premiere back in the nineties; she waved and exposed her abundant beauty of brown pit hair, and everyone lost it. Like, literally lost their shit. It made headline news.

HEADLINE FUCKING NEWS that a woman dared to wave and not shave her armpits. WHAT THE FUCKETY FUCKING FUCK is that about? So, we wonder why we feel this rage, and fear of being bold? Because it is lightly sprinkled with heavy shame . . . with rejection. We don't get to own the idea of letting that shame go. And don't get me wrong, I know men feel shame on a completely different level, I understand they have struggles too – no one is even debating that – but the truth is women are continually shamed for how they look. We don't often get to make our own choices over what we want because then you're labelled wild-eyed and eccentric, like that woman who has dreads, wears flowery yoga pants and smells like an onion that rotted inside a camel's bumhole. Body hair is the most natural thing we could own, and yet I still find myself removing it just to make sure I am more pleasing on the eye. I don't want to fucking remove it because I am desperate to not give a fuck what society says about how my body looks, but I am not there yet. Is this a conscious realisation? Nope! And yet I do know deep down I don't own the balls to wear the dress and let my leg hair flap in the wind without a care in the world.

BODY HAIR, I DON'T CARE – but the patri-archy does . . . I know you don't want to hear it, but the body hair hang-up is part of the beauty standards set by men a really long time ago. Like, before we were born and still hanging around like a bad smell. Did you know that Mr Gillette learned he could double his profits all that way back when by telling women to shave to fit in with the latest fashion trend of dresses? Bang, and thus began your New Age thing of shaving your body to within an inch of its life. Women now spend more time removing hair all thanks to the orig-inal brain spasm of a . . . man. I am sorry to be the person to break this to you if you've never been told this before; I understand it could be potentially rough to hear. I felt pretty pissed about it too when I realised. Why do we wax and shave everything to oblivion? Because we are surrounded by women who don't show hair. I recently did a photo shoot – for this book, in fact; you'll most definitely know the photo . . . well, because it'll be in here somewhere – and I had let my armpits grow out. Like, I could brush the hair long. I felt nervous to allow other women to see it. NERV-OUS?? Over armpit hair!! ME?? Yes, me!! I realised in that moment, as I openly and loudly admitted to not shaving, that I was nervous. Thankfully I was in the presence of strong, empowered women, and they really didn't give a shit, and for that I was thankful.

How many of you can openly hold your hands up and say you have left your body hair to grow naturally with complete conviction and no shame? I have this really dark feeling it'll be next to none of you. Not because you aren't the strong feminist I know you are, but because of how you've been judged for it. I have myself felt like women who don't keep up with shaving were dirty, or unkempt. Obvs, I don't feel that way any more but in my twenties I could never have entertained the idea of leaving my armpit hair beyond two days. Is it because as I get older I care less? Maybe, but I see plenty of women in their fifties, sixties and beyond still maintaining that standard. So, while I would like to think my beliefs have changed because I care less, it is actually much more down to challenging the way I think and unlearning what has been taught to me from as young as a baby.

Do we need the entire world to fit into our ideals of women? No! I still shave, I still enjoy a bikini wax (enjoy is probably a stretch). I am still doing it, mainly because I'm not there yet; I am not fully accepting of my whole entire natural hairy body and what it looks like, but I'm working on it. I love that phrase, 'I'm working on it'; like it's giving you permission to just be who you are in that moment and not be too harsh on yourself for all the things you've not managed to achieve yet, like growing out your minge hair and plaiting it – I'm working on it. Told you – it was one hell of a rant, wasn't it!

The women we are expected to be aren't the women we are supposed to be. We grow hair, we fart, we wee, we shit, we get bloated, we get PMS, we suffer the highs and lows of our hormones, which, honest to God, aren't ever given the credit they deserve. We have so much of society to blame for that, for the filters on social media, the photoshopping of magazine covers, and for porn.

The thing that grips my shit more often than not is the idea that to be a feminist you should fit inside this stereotype. The hate I see on social media from other women bashing fellow women for maybe fucking shaving their bikini line and actively talking about feminism pisses me off. HOW can you effectively support women but only support the women who fit your mindset? DON'T DO THAT!! The whole point of being a feminist is to talk about the issues women face daily, so marginalising the voices of those who should be allowed to speak up completely negates the point of using our voices. Allow women to share their experiences, career, choices and bodies without expecting them to fit inside another set of bloody ideals.

There is so much designed for men, and it's been there for generation upon generation, that it's hard to separate out which is which. Porn being one of those many things; it's just always been generalised as for men. There is some really beautifully directed porn out there (usually directed by women) that can be so real and sensual without it needing to be a massive cum shot over a girl's back, and yet when you think of porn, that's more than likely what your mind goes to. The completely unrealistic way men and women are expected to perform during sex. The way women are portrayed as behaving in the bedroom means we're all completely falsely alerted to what it 'should' look like, and how it should sound. Teen boys are using it as a personal guide of how to do it and how to treat a woman, and with dangerous pornography easily accessible across the internet – which, by the way, sees girls having to rely on the legal system to remove videos of them being raped – we are pumping out this really fucking deluded idea that women come at the same time as men, with next to no clit stimulation and a broken fucking washing machine that needs repairing.

Porn has its place, but it's the really outdated 'quick fuck, girl gets turned on by guy with moustache at front door holding a spanner' kind of porn that is not only blindsiding both sexes with what to expect in the bedroom but also what they should look like.

I don't like a bare beaver – I am more retro bush – and yet it's slug lips central across a lot of porn because that's what a lot of men like to see. Why are our bodies and how they look, or how we look after them, still up for a man's approval? Meanwhile, women are expecting someone with a 19-inch dick to make them wet when in actual fact it's probably just going to give you a urine infection and tonsillitis at the same time. We all fanny fart, even if we don't want to admit it; sometimes that happens, and sometimes we might even have a smelly crack because the heat of the moment meant you didn't have time to wash. It is awkward, it is embarrassing because no one wants that experience during something sexual, but it is real. It is life, it's how we all look and how we all live, but apparently we would prefer to uphold that really toxic, unrealistic look instead of being a woman who gets what she wants in the bedroom, or is given a choice over how her body might naturally feel or react during sex, because we're still so wrapped up in this idea that men are the priority in any sexual experience. I can only speak for myself there, but I can say that in my late teens, into my early twenties, I didn't know how to confidently demand what I wanted sexually because this very idea of pleasing a man dominated anything else I needed for myself. I was so concerned with making all the noises, doing the moves, and all the while I'd be inwardly thinking about what to have for dinner or avoiding angles that gave me a double chin.

I think Steve has seen every double chin and ring of my arsehole now and I've realised from being in a good relationship that he wants to see me genuinely enjoy the experience – with my retro bush, hairy armpits and donkey grunting – because I'm having a fucking good time. That is the kind of porn that everyone needs to see (this is not me telling you that my next professional move is into porn, by the way). And it doesn't only happen in porn either; in nearly every single Hollywood sex scene, we see women happily orgasm via a wide shaft and a 20-second romp. There is no realistic portrayal out there of what sex really looks like, which seems odd because we all just seem to enjoy watching very unrealistic experiences and then shame ourselves for never living up to the thing even the movie stars can't manage.

NO SHAME

We need to empower each other in our experiences of sex, and body hair and piles. It feels so taboo to admit you need a shit on the way back from the school run and I just don't see why?? We all do it. At some point, in whatever way it might come out, we all shit. Ladies don't talk about that, though, and the shame of admitting it is like a step too far. I don't think we've ever really been good at empowering each other or passing the mic to someone who has something different to say. We struggle with allowing a difference of opinion mainly because we feel attacked, and yet I've been able to have really grown-up, mature conversations with some of my bestest friends over things we can't agree on that haven't ended in an argument. It's just sometimes okay to listen and not judge for whatever is coming out of their mouths. It's hard, though, because you need to be secure enough in your own life and decisions to hold your convictions and not let a conversation make you feel threatened.

While I love being a woman, and I adore the women in my life, I recognise the fact we are bitchy as fuck. We like to throw around this whole freedom of speech bullshit to each other because we just think our voices count on everything. Sometimes, they just don't. Sometimes we just have to ssshhhhh and let that person say or feel whatever the hell they're thinking. It's called validating. We can't expect others to hear us or validate us if we can't do that for ourselves. And finding people who will validate you is part of a process of once again believing enough in yourself to surround yourself with the people who truly love and cherish you enough to hear you and not suggest that whatever you're feeling is wrong or should be changed. This is called manipulating and it can easily be mistaken for empowering, but it's not. It's actually incredibly damaging and dangerous. Why? Because it is fitting other people into our own agenda. I have been in too many situations like this in my life, and I think, because in many ways I have felt like the person with the weaker personality, that I was more easily swayed and just agreed. I might not have really agreed, but I have just wanted to fit in. As I type this I think, *But what if people who know me disagree with this idea of me?* LAURA, STOP. It doesn't matter what they think; they are not you and you are allowed to own this idea and know it's actually okay to say to the world, 'I have let other people manipulate how I have seen situations.'

Well, what are we waiting for? Where is my posse of pussies to help us get to the top? Why are we all fighting for the same thing on our own? I have seen first-hand the cut-throat behaviour of women around other women in business. It is ruthless, and I believe a lot of that comes down to the fact we see, hear and absorb how few women make it to the same realms of men. So, when you have finally staggered onto the ladder and continue to fight harder than a man to be heard, respected or even valued, then the mentality is: *Fuck no, I'm not helping another woman to get here because she could threaten everything I have worked my arse off for. She could be my competition; she could be my direct threat.*

I have seen women take jobs from other women because they are that fucking harsh that they will stop at nothing to be the person who redirects the attention to them. We are born into a society that expects so much of women and we become so singular in how we behave, even from childhood. You generally see girls demanding they do things on their own, boys less so. They are happy to have things done for them, and I see that with my own children. I have heard people talk about how they treat their boys differently to their girls. I appreciate that honesty and upfront reflection on how they parent. So, is that a nature or nurture response – the way girls will generally just get on with things and boys are quite happy to sit back and let it be done for them? I honestly don't have the answer. We learn from our surroundings and we often lose our community in among the fear of admitting we need help.

I am shit at asking for help. It feels like a direct attack on my own ability as a woman. So I instead struggle, again something I am working on because I am realising the people around me want nothing but the best for me. And so, if I reach out for help, I do know now that for the first time in my life I will be met with a loving hand to help me. See, I told you I got me a pussy posse.

I can't say it's a walk in the park, but it's more leaning into the idea I can just speak about the things I feel like I need to share and feel safe enough to do it. I don't know if it's something I have to work on for the rest of my life, because I haven't got the conviction to say that, if I find myself very vulnerable again, I won't shut down as that appears to annoyingly be my knee-jerk reaction to life. I have spoken to some of my friends this year for the first time to tell them I was sexually abused and it felt really hard and heavy to do. I felt terrified they would judge me or even wonder why I was still having a problem with it. (Believe it or not, that's actually something I have previously been told.) It has taken a lot of guts, but I've done it for me because I needed to share it and not be so afraid of their reaction. I've told people in the past and felt let down by how they chose to respond. The difference I have noticed with telling the right people is that they just listened. They simply passed me the mic and didn't expect me to behave or respond in a way that made them feel good. They just were . . . completely there.

These are the women we need; they're the right ones for me. It's always going to be okay to say no to friendships; it's always going to be okay to enforce your own boundaries and it's going to be completely acceptable to sometimes say FUCK OFF. You aren't a robot, you aren't made to make the most perfect decisions and sometimes you're going to need to say sorry. That's healthy; it's okay to be reflective enough that you see when you've done wrong.

You have come so far, so why waste the rest of your life on awful wine, cheap chocolate and terrible friendships? (For the record, if you're ever coming to my house, I do actually like cheap chocolate.)

You just want your version of happiness and friendship. What does that look like? What is your tick list? How does it feel? What makes you feel safe, or loved?

The things we need aren't ever going to be the same and you're going to sometimes grow up or out of things you didn't expect, but sometimes it's your brain's way of telling you it's time to move on – not up; we don't exit friendships acting like a cunt. We exit knowing we have our integrity, or at least some of it. If someone is expecting you to expertly execute this, then they are expecting something even they can't achieve.

We all have our own version of events, we all have our own desires to show that we aren't at fault and we all want to do everything we can to just be able to say, 'I did nothing wrong.' It makes us sleep easier at night, I think. Just let it be, and resist the need to justify your actions, your responses or your reasons. You don't need to give them enough chapters to make a novel; you just need to give them enough to find the ending. Even if it's not the one they were looking for.

Thank you to all the bad-ass feminist bitches out there that continue to support women, pass the mic and also step away when they're strong enough to recognise when it's time to move on. We all have our superpowers and, much like the beautiful story about everyone having a soul mate out there somewhere, I do believe that about friendships and women.

This chapter has felt quite heavy in damning women into saying we aren't particularly supportive of each other and at any given opportunity we stab each other in the back. I wouldn't be where I am or who I am without the strong women in my life. They're the ones who have trusted me to be there in their lowest moments, who haven't felt like they have to float through life like nothing hurts or impacts them. They're the women who have just given me so much time, love and support, and they are also the people I have learned to be vulnerable around because they as my friends have given me a safe space to do so. I once went to a yoga class and cried. I go every Monday with my friend who I've known since I was four. I walked back to the car and I just cried; I just didn't even understand why but I was in this feeling of real vulnerability and she just allowed me to be who- ever I needed to be. I don't know that I really had a direct, obvious reason to cry, I just felt so overwhelmed by life.

That moment has stuck for me; it's stuck really hard because I have felt so mortified when I have shown emotions in front of others that I've felt this overwhelming need to say sorry. She didn't want me to be sorry; she just got the fact I needed that moment and didn't try to change it or suppress it.

So, yes, women have a lot to learn in the way of supporting each other, but I think what it really comes down to is making sure the people you allow around you are the ones that just make you feel okay. They aren't expecting you to show up all-singing, all-dancing; they just want you to show up okay. They want you to give them the version of yourself you feel strong enough to give, and sometimes that's the one that cracks jokes and other times it's the one who just doesn't want to be brave.

I love the women in my life. They have taught me a lot about myself, even the shitty experiences where I have had to let go have been a lesson in what I want or even deserve for myself. And of course there have been the moments where maybe I haven't been the best version of myself and had to come with my tail between my legs and say sorry. Those experiences, as horrible as they are to feel, they are still a really important life lesson to learn and grow from.

We are surviving in a world that believes it wasn't designed for us and so that kind of makes it a cock-fest to navigate. It means everything we are is questioned, and we're pitted against each other like a pack of lions ripping apart its prey.

So be sure to remember your fellow woman, support her as you go and let's prove to ourselves why we matter and how this world would literally be fucked without us. Simple fact!

CHAPTER 5

Self-Care and Self-Esteem

Self-care is such a hugely important part of our lives and yet we aren't regularly taught about its benefits.

Life is busy and the demand to be more and more present is ever-increasing. Our overall happiness is at an all-time low thanks to that fucking pandemic, and we're all trying really hard to figure how the fuck we are meant to implement something we don't actually know how to do. Why don't we know how to do it? Because we are raised with examples of women who often don't stop, and who very rarely address their own needs. We learn self-care through what we see others doing around us, and most of us don't grow up with that model.

We often don't feel entitled to what we have. We really struggle to own why we got it and others didn't. I think deep down we just want to fit in, we want people around us to make us feel accepted. So, when something comes along that's good, it feels at times a bit like we don't deserve it, or like we haven't earned it, so we spend our lives trying to justify why we should have it. We shouldn't have to do that.

I am the first person to admit I get this overwhelming, bumhole-stretching feeling whenever I am going away on holiday, and that I should dumb down why we might be having it. Our honeymoon, for instance. We went to the Maldives. I'll be honest, it was pretty fucking lovely. It was 12 years ago and even now, all these years later, I will quickly tell people the only reason we could afford that holiday was because I had been involved in a car accident and the insurance payout paid for the holiday. What a twat! Instead of saying it was beautiful and actually we just deserved it, I go into the fucking backstory over why we only managed this holiday because we were the poor people who won the Willy Wonka golden ticket. Truth was, we were both in good jobs, and come hell or high fucking water I was going to the Maldives on my honeymoon, even if it meant it went on a credit card. I let the guilt of the holiday I felt I didn't really deserve take over. The fact I had a nice fucking honeymoon and admitting that and saying I had a wonderful time doesn't make me a bragging cunt.

That holiday was self-care; it was beautiful, and glamorous and the most fucking relaxing time of my life where I had no fucking kids and I could have sex with my husband in the day and not have to whisper. That might not have been someone else's honeymoon and that might well be a sticking point for them that they didn't manage something as wonderful, but that isn't my fucking problem – meant in the least 'I don't give a shit' way possible.

The bottom line is we are allowed the nice things, without the shitty guilt and gut-wrenching shame that we don't deserve it. We don't have to keep quiet about how we afforded the new car, or the new wardrobe, or take the shine off of going out on a date with our husband because we were able to afford a babysitter. We have to stop doing this!

'How?' I hear you cry in dismay. You have to know and believe we are allowed it. Again, you're like, 'Tell me something I don't fucking know, Laura!!' Well, in my humble opinion of absolute fucking greatness, I believe you manage that through working on your self-esteem.

I never realised I suffered with low self-esteem until I started reading about it. I ticked all the boxes. Would you like to know what low self-esteem looks like? Well, my friends, look no further; I will provide you with the details right here:

- Lack of confidence
- Self-comparison (not the good kind)
- Struggling to ask for what you want or need
- Fear of failure
- Negative self-talk
- Finding it impossible to just accept a compliment
- Worry and self-doubt
- Poor boundaries
- People-pleasing

All of the above are pretty broad and there are other characteristics that go into shitty self-esteem but these guys were power-jumping, high-fiving the shit out of my life, and I had literally no idea. I knew I struggled to accept compliments; I knew I had really awful self-doubt, but I had no idea that was what low self-esteem looked like. If you've just read the above and gone, 'Well, fuck me! That's me too!' that makes me feel massively better about the fact I have been pretty fucking ignorant to something I have been telling women to work on for years while having no idea I, too, was that woman.

Where do you even fucking begin to tackle something that big? Well, we start small and we don't give up because, once we believe more in ourselves, we won't feel so much like we're robbing someone of their joy when good things are already happening to us. We will learn to accept the good things that happen are because we are worthy of them, and ultimately I'd like to think you'll just feel happier.

I can say this quite confidently because if there is one thing I have massively focused on this year with a real sense of importance it's been my self-esteem. It has been so shockingly low that I very rarely said anything nice to myself. I instead would label myself a failure who just didn't get anything right. I couldn't ever see any positive in myself unless someone told me and, while I loved the pat on the head, I also felt this really huge need to push away the compliment for fear of being seen as big-headed or too cocky.

We shouldn't ever say these things to women. Men are allowed to believe in themselves, but women are more often than not given really shit labels when we display the same attitudes as men. Yes, men are, in fact, as likely to suffer with low self-esteem, but I will just remind you that I can't write this book with the experience of a man from a male's point of view. I can, however, confirm a man is much more readily accepted for being confident than a woman is.

The first thing I started with was my negative self-talk; it was literally corroding away my life. I felt like the biggest stick of shit in life. I realised through reading that no level of medication or waiting for things to improve would actually make that better. I had to start now, I had to do it myself. I couldn't let the words of other people dictate my life. I couldn't rely on them saying I was good enough to actually believe in myself.

I would strive for perfection in how I lived my life, but I never achieved it because my level or version of perfection was unachievable. I felt like if I cried I was weak, if I lost my shit I was a bad person and if I felt hurt by someone else's words I was pathetic. I would torture myself internally over and over again for being all these really awful things: weak, horrible and pathetic.

Can you see how something as small as labelling normal, natural reactions as negative can be so corruptive in your own life? Those small words grow into much bigger ideas the more you feed them. I wanted to be the person who had it all together and I didn't know why things like crying were getting in the way of me living my best life.

We aren't fucking robots! We aren't designed to not feel. We aren't designed to not make mistakes either. How can anyone grow without making mistakes along the way? The only thing I have gained from criticising myself for all the things I have less than perfectly showed up for is a detrimental dent in my mental health. I have punished myself and told myself I'm a failure.

Being able to speak more kindly to myself has given me the space to grow emotionally; it has given me the opportunity to just breathe, accept and move on. Move on from the hurt and pain I have caused myself, saying, 'It's okay.'

I would like to give some examples of the inner conversations I would and still have and what I have done to turn them around:

'But what if I can't?' → 'But what if I can?'

This sounds like quite a trivial one, but how often do your thoughts start with *But what if I can't*? It could be going on a date, or going to do the food shop, or looking after the kids alone. It could be so many things that make you inwardly think, *But what if I can't*? Yet the simple power of changing that statement to *But what if I can do it*? carries so much weight. It is okay to be scared; it's okay for it to feel overwhelming. Every single time your brain says, *But what if I can't*? just answer back KINDLY with *But what if I can*? So what if you are internally saying it to yourself 60 times a day. Eventually you will start to believe it.

'I wish I was someone else.' → 'Look at how kind and wonderful I am.'

This feels really huge for me. It has been this level of self-comparison as mentioned earlier in the book that has robbed me of so many moments of happiness. I have believed that if I was someone else, I'd be happier or stronger; that I wouldn't struggle with my mental health like I do. I have always believed that confidence and a positive image of yourself is a thing you either have or don't have. Like, it never takes work, it's just something you're almost born with. That you are stuck with the mindset you have. I realise now that your mindset is always going to be changing, and learning to accept the good things about who you are is perfectly acceptable, not to mention totally healthy too. I love who I am: I am caring and kind; I am sweet and considerate; I am wonderful and worthy. As I have repeated these things to myself over and over again, most days I have imagined all the times I have been that person who has been kind, caring, loving and sweet. To begin with it felt alien and I would quickly go back to all the times I'd fucked up and ruined things, or was a bad person. It felt really hard, like this conflicting area in my brain just couldn't accept the fact she was actually a good person. But I stayed with it, and now that process has become easier. Dwelling on things like not being as good as someone else has eased and I am learning to be better at letting go of this idea.

'I deserve to be treated like that.' → 'NAH, mate, you don't.'

I have been pretty good at completely neglecting my own needs to fulfil others'. I have done it all of my life, which, as I've already said, completely fits the MO of someone who has been abused. The fear of being abandoned by people we believe we need to survive means we allow ourselves to continually be abused because we are fucked without them.

We do not deserve to be treated like shit. End of story. If the toxic relationship makes you question your worth, your goodness or your reality then kindly step the fuck out and wish them well. You don't need them but you do need to believe you can survive without them. For me, it was the fear of what they might tell others. *What if they turn everyone against me?* Hello, abandonment issues; I see you again.

'This will make them happy.' → 'Does it make me happy?'

If you are a people-pleaser it is exceptionally hard to accept the crushing truth that you don't need to please everyone. You don't need to keep putting yourself last. Happiness comes from being happy for yourself, not just others. You don't need to show up and be counted every time to be considered a good person. I have personally found that when others have told me about how they might have been let down by me, and talked about past experiences where I wasn't up to their standard of friendship, I have taken that so personally that I have only worked harder at pleasing them and rejecting any of my needs. I have completely overlooked myself because it feels like such a personal attack to be accused of caring for myself, rather than turning the tables on the person who has selfishly expected something from me I clearly couldn't give at that time.

'I don't believe I am strong enough.' → 'I am going to give it a try.'

I think the word 'strong' brings up a lot of things that don't actually represent strength. The person we think of as 'strong' is more often than not someone who doesn't really show struggle or emotions. They appear to take life in their stride. I have never been that person and for the very few times I have managed to take things in my stride, I have later gone on to have a breakdown, so actually, I still don't believe it's a reasonable thing to ask someone to show strength by being emotionless over struggle or pain.

I waited and waited for my strength to arrive like the bus that was running late. I almost thought if I stood at the side of the road it would just arrive and I could jump on it and leave the past behind. Actually, the only way to summon that strength and show myself I very much had it was to face the things that made me feel weak. I had to really challenge my reasons for not wanting to do something and ask myself whether they actually came down to me believing I wasn't strong enough! I used to think that maybe if I waited a little longer and fixed myself a little more in therapy, these things, like being able to take the dog for a walk, would just come back. But in my personal experiences of reintroducing things into my life that scared me, no amount of time removed the fear. I had to prove to myself why I could do them.

Another thing that has been really transformative for me to use in how I approach and arrive at myself is positive affirmations. In the early days of my latest mental catastrophe, I would google affirmations and they would provide me with comfort, but because I lacked so much confidence in who I was, I couldn't hold on to what I was reading. I was too weak, too scared, too tired, too self-doubting to manage any form of acceptance that those words of comfort just needed a little more time in my brain. Really, I just needed to sit with them for longer, to give them a bit of room to get comfortable and stick around.

I would beat myself up for not keeping an affirmation's positive feeling and I would assume I was getting even that wrong. I stopped looking at them because I labelled myself stupid for thinking they would even work! After a period of time, though, after reading more about how to overcome poor self-esteem, I realised they were actually really valuable. I looked at them with new vigour and realised that all the warm things I felt when I read them were actually really powerful and important, and I allowed myself to cling to them and use them daily when things were just feeling really overwhelming.

Here are some affirmations that helped me:

- 'I won't give up on you, so don't give up on me.'
- 'I'm doing my best.'
- 'I am going to get through this.'
- 'I am so kind.'

- 'I am loving and giving.'
- 'I am worthy of good things.'
- 'I am brave and I am strong.'
- 'I forgive myself.'
- 'I am enough.'
- 'I can overcome every challenge I face.'

These were and still are some of my favourites, the top one being the most prominent because it came during a time where I really felt out of control with my thoughts. They hurt to even think about and so there were times when all I felt like I had was this other person in my life, fighting like hell to keep me going: Steve. So I just kept saying, 'I won't give up on you, so don't give up on me' to him, over and over. I would often sob as I said it and he would kind of sit there, probably thinking, *Will you stop saying the same fucking thing over and over?* These things people make up, the things they say, they become little pockets to give strength and hope in a way they don't even realise. They give people the chance to feel less alone.

We all know we aren't alone in our struggles, and yet they still feel so isolating when we are in them because most people we are around aren't suffering like we are in that moment. These little anecdotes scattered across places like Google are lifelines for when you feel like you have nowhere else to turn to change how you feel about yourself.

This whole idea that you learn it and then leave it is actually an idea someone, somewhere, came up with to make you believe there is an end to it all. I actually don't know if I want to find the end; I live in fear that the moment I think I don't need to work on my self-worth any more is the moment when I start slipping backwards. Obviously that is much more dramatic than it is in reality but the evidence is there; the proof is in the things we read and listen to. You can't ever stop working on yourself because all the time you are growing, you are changing, and the most important job you could do for yourself is to continue to adapt and change with that person constantly evolving within you.

Now, can you see how impossibly difficult it must be to provide yourself with any form of care when this is the conversation that goes on in your head? The fact we believe the people who love their lives a little more are a world away from who we are because we don't have what they have to succeed or just be happy? We could well be that happy, contented person and actually that's really refreshing to think because it shows it's achievable, that those things aren't another world away. They are within you, but you need to identify what it is about how you speak to yourself that makes you fail to access it. Even down to the hairdresser's; I have refused to allow myself a haircut. Not because we couldn't afford it, but because I felt like it was unnecessary. I would manage to convince myself I didn't really need it, that things weren't so bad that I had to actually pay to have a haircut. Why did I need one? To make myself feel good? How selfish! That is how I saw myself, a selfish cowbag for believing she needed a haircut, because I felt I should just be grateful for what I've got and not need any form of additional help to be happy.

A fucking haircut.

A FUCKING HAIRCUT and I told myself I was selfish for even thinking I deserved it. Now, I have my hair done every five weeks; I've even shaved some of it off. It has been met with mixed reviews, with some people saying they like it, and others that they aren't sure on it. I have for the first time in my entire life, with my hand on my heart, not needed their approval and not worried about the fact they might not like what I did with my hair. Because it is mine. I feel empowered by myself for knowing I am allowed this for me. I don't need others to tell me it was a good idea; I have just lived and breathed my own happiness for doing it. Why? Because I fucking deserve it. I deserve to make choices for myself and not let someone else's opinion sway me like it would have done before. I have come to realise my self-care and self-esteem is so tightly caught up with public opinion and how I'm expected to be seen that I stopped existing for myself and started existing for everyone else.

In fact, when I think about it, I don't really know if I've ever just existed for me? Have you? Can you think of a time when you positively put yourself first and felt confident you were entitled to it? Have you ever just spoken to yourself with such love and compassion that you've fallen in love with who you are?

We are allowed to be in love with ourselves. It isn't some mighty declaration of love where you marry yourself, but it most definitely means you should have a honeymoon with yourself! You should love how your body feels; you should enjoy the places it takes you and you should worship it.

Which leads me on to self-pleasure. I can already feel some of you shift in your seats with awkwardness because that word feels dirty. It did for me for many years, well into my twenties. I didn't actually know that masturbation was for women. I know that sounds fucking ridiculous but I just didn't.

So, is it a part of self-care? Absolutely. I remember going to Ann Summers in my twenties; I had never been in there. I was a nervous wreck and I hoped I didn't look like someone who didn't belong. I had up until that point never owned a sex toy. I grabbed a vibrating cock ring, and the famous rampant rabbit. I raced home, so excited to be alone in the house Steve and I rented to try the pink pleasure wand. I had been having sex for a good few years and yet I had never really known what an orgasm really felt like unless Steve was giving my clit a good old talking-to. I hadn't ever touched it, unless to wipe it. Self-pleasure actually felt sinful, which is weird because I am not actually a religious person, and yet that's the best way to describe it. Being a survivor of abuse, I think, fits with why I never felt like I should pleasure myself because it seemed wrong and that I was a disgusting person for doing it.

Anyway, I get home, leg it up the stairs, barely able to get my trousers undone fast enough, flinging the shitty plastic packaging to the floor and off I went . . . Oh. Okay. It feels alright!! I guess, but actually I can't say this is a porno moment where I'm squirting on the ceiling . . . The tiny balls inside the shaft are making a whirling sound that is close to listening to my nan's arthritic fingers clicking and it's drying up my clit faster than a hairdryer to my face, but it still kind of felt nice . . . but the big wow was lost on me. GUTTED.

I can't even tell you why I decided to use the cock ring. I did, though; I just gave it a go, without a cock to put in it, and FUCK ME. I don't know if my neighbours heard but I was too busy buzzing my clit off to care. I remember excitedly collecting Steve from work and saying, 'OH MY GOD, you wait until you get home.' That was my introduction to self-pleasure and yet it has taken well into my thirties to not feel shame over admitting I like to masturbate, and I am allowed to do it alone.

It has really felt like an uncommonly known, undis-covered fact that part of our self-discovery is through loving our own body enough to know how to make it feel good. I used to feel so embarrassed for even sug-gesting a sex toy during sex, like I wasn't allowed that. Even as I write this now there is this voice that says to me, 'Laura, should you really be saying this? Think of your children.' Why is it I have to think of my children when I openly discuss female pleasure and yet the discussion of men wanking has always been widely known and perfectly welcomed into everyday life? I have heard a million jokes about men having a little tug and yet can you imagine what a conversation killer it would be for a woman to say the same thing? WHAT?!!

I don't understand how we haven't contested this issue more. How something so beautiful (it is) can be so horrifically snubbed, or considered a 'man thing'. In no way am I wanting to print these words to make a man feel turned on, and nor should they. It's just a basic fact; women are also sexual beings and not just for the satisfaction of their partners.

I'm not suggesting that you have one off with yourself and it'll all just be wonderful and happy, but I am saying that as women we are entitled to it without the shame or embarrassment. I regret not enforcing my own pleasure first in my relationship and that isn't the fault of any partner I've been with; it's more the fact I have been that inexperienced in myself that I just didn't know what I was doing or what I was even allowed to do. How insane! To even believe I needed permission to touch my minge, and yet that's exactly what it felt like. Like, no one explained it and I just didn't know what to do, so I assumed I wasn't meant to experience the kind of sex you saw in the movies, which involved no fanny farts or clit stimulation and ended with an orgasm every time.

The thing about self-care means you can be allowed to explore yourself without the permission of someone else and you are allowed to enjoy it without feeling wrong for it. Self-esteem means sometimes you are allowed to put yourself first in sex without feeling like you aren't entitled to it, but there also needs to be a level of confidence you have to find in yourself if you've never learned to ask for it.

I am in a healthy relationship and have been for 20 years, and even I've struggled with having that conversation with my husband. I don't want to dress this up to be a wonderful conversation over wine and a takeaway. You just have to work off of the basis that you do deserve to have the sexual experience you read about, with the help of a sex toy or not, and you should always expect to be met with complete acceptance and approval. If the idea of a sex toy threatens your partner's ego, well, quite frankly that is absolutely not fucking acceptable.

'Owning ourselves' feels like a weirdly possessive thing to say but it is the only way I can really describe it. I have had to fight so hard to own myself in a healthy way that doesn't negatively dominate everything I think about myself.

You have to start small but above all else you have to be kind with it. Beating yourself up only continues to drive this idea you are a failure or you aren't worthy. Sometimes we are going to have bad days, where we feel like our brain has wanted to completely make everything feel dark. Although those days suck, they are also okay. It is just okay to feel those days.

Nothing in life is ever straightforward and fighting for our own identity while managing a life of work, parenting, relationships and a home is hard. Don't go so hard on yourself for all the things emotionally you haven't achieved.

I'd like to end with this: Have you heard we're awesome? I know!! CAN YOU EVEN BELIEVE IT?!!? WE. ARE. AWESOME!! We just forget to tell ourselves. So, we continue on this whole 'I must do more to be accepted' inner chat. We know our internal monologue can be pretty fucking depressing to hear. If we allowed our inner thoughts to be external – like if I were queueing in the bank to cash a cheque and I told myself 'I am disgusting and wish I could lose weight' – if they were said aloud for all to hear, would we actually say those words??

Chances are nope, not a fucking chance. We would say all the things we would want people to think about us. Like, 'I am really kind', 'I am amazing at blow jobs', 'I am a kick-ass mum' . . . We want people to see how amazing we are. So, it's about time we started turning that chat around to ourselves. We don't need to be patted on the head and told how good we are doing by someone else; we need to learn to do it for ourselves. We are surviving all these little moments and never, ever taking a moment to just celebrate how amazing that makes us. We are so strong, capable and remarkable, and we have to repeat those words over and over again because they are one of the biggest tools we could ever teach ourselves.

Every morning when you wake up, think of something kind about you, something about YOU that makes you amazing. Anything! You don't need to write these thoughts down if you don't want to. There are no rules; this is your list of awesome reasons why you rock.

Fill in the blanks: what are you?

I am . . .

I am . . .

I am . . .

I am . . .

AND the challenge is you're not allowed to make these 'I am' statements negative. They are only allowed to point out something awesome about yourself. Keep doing it, because the reality is it won't hurt. Keep knowing that for every 'I am', those little words will have a positive impact.

We don't need to believe the negative things we say about ourselves. They are often there because we've been hurt and we want to avoid being hurt again, while hurting ourselves with self-deprecating worth-lessness. You aren't a planet and solar system away from just loving yourself more. The whole 'we are what we eat' idea can also be changed for 'we are what we say about ourselves'.

Speaking of what we eat, diet is a huge multi-billion-pound industry and its whole job is to pry into your insecurities, find them, make you feel bad about them and then change them. This has a massively huge impact on our self-esteem, which can then lead to extreme eating habits such as binge eating or starving ourselves. Every time you show up to one of those classes and stand on those scales seeing what you weigh, just know the entire premise of that class is to shame you into believing you either need to lose more weight or that you've failed because you gained it.

At some point or another, the restricted calorie intake or carb-free diet is going to see you fall on your arse. Not because of anything other than the idea that this is a lifestyle change is a pile of bullshit. We congratulate people for being 'slimmer of the month' or even of the year, and we never, ever celebrate the woman who continues to try and struggles with the balance between real life and weight loss. It is fucking tragic and I find myself biting my tongue whenever I hear women say 'I really need to start dieting' because those diets are all designed to do one thing: make you feel like without it, you will fail. They want you to believe you are literally only ever going to find happiness if you lose two stone. I hear it and you must too. I hear the person who says, 'I will just be happier if I get down to this dress size or that weight.'

I have always openly expressed the fact I don't own scales, because I deserve better than to stand on them and be defined by the number that appears. How can you change an issue as big as diet when even doctor's surgeries hand out coupons for local weight-loss groups you can attend for free? That is our answer. 'You are fat; you must go here to have your answers solved through sitting in a room full of people who also feel like utter shit and see who weighs more than you while everyone discusses how they promise to be good next week.'

As soon as the thing, the food that brings you more joy than an orgasm, touches your lips, what will you do during or even after that experience? Do you pat yourself on the back and say, 'Well done, that was bloody enjoyable'? Do you fuck! You make yourself feel like shit for being weak, gross, disgusting or fat. You hate yourself, and there we have again the negative shitty chat of 'I hate myself', 'I should know better', 'I am not good enough', and that really angry, unhappy person takes hold of you and says that, in the eyes of society, you're 'failing'. We see ourselves through the things we watch, read and listen to and who we hang around with. I know I have at points in my life felt so insecure about my weight gain and looked for positive reinforcement from others. But actually, because I never believed them, those responses only heightened that shitty little voice of doom telling me I was fat. I was looking in all the wrong places for that affirmation when *I* should have been the person talking kindly to myself about my body.

I appreciate dieting is there for a good reason, but does it include cutting everything out and replacing it with a shake that is so packed full of shit that doesn't even remotely begin with anything natural and kills your soul slowly because it doesn't allow for cheese or chocolate? No, it doesn't! It's about approaching diet, your diet, your lifestyle, with – once again – kindness. We all know fast food is not good food, we all know no one could live on it long term without health issues, and we all know it is full of the shit we really shouldn't consume. Does that stop me sitting at the drive-thru on a Friday night waiting to collect my order? Does it fuck. Sometimes our need to eat comes from a place of comfort. We need comfort, but why are we choosing to comfort ourselves with food? Is it because of something from childhood? Does it come from trauma? Does it come from hurt?

I am not here to tell you that all diets should be banned – there is literally no point in even trying to attempt that. It is a completely wasted idea that it would even work, but I do hope you will read this and realise you aren't actually meant to want to lose weight and punish yourself for it in the process.

Why did I allow myself to get this big? Why did I just eat that? How come they lost more weight than me? When will I get to my goal? Look back at those statements. Can you see how you've probably said one of those to yourself at least once? I imagine you can, and what I see when I look at them is a lot of whys and whens. So the questions I think would be far more valuable to ask are: *Why do I see myself as a failure? When will I change the way I speak to myself? How can I start?* That all sounds a lot gentler and kinder. Every time the angry, frustrated how, when or why kicks in, why don't you try turning them on their head to find more nourishing solutions to what your goals really look like. I don't know those answers, because they're unique to the individual, but one thing I can promise is those answers are most definitely somewhere within you.

You need to find balance, by which I mean the balance between finding food that'll nourish your body and soul and emotionally checking in with how you're feeling. For me, what time of the month it is will dictate how much I crave sugar. I don't want to punish myself for eating it, I just need it and, the more I resist that, the shittier I become, not just with myself but everyone around me.

Last time I checked I was just over 13 and a half stone, I am five foot ten and I am considered overweight. I probably do need to lose a few pounds, but emotionally I am not able to commit to that idea. I understand the fact right now my body is already battling the mental load of recovering from a breakdown, and I can't start to consume myself with the idea a doctor could potentially shame me for needing to lose weight.

Our emotional well-being is never, ever taken into consideration when we want to lose weight. *Where am I at emotionally? Do things feel heavy?* Yeah, they do! Actually for me they feel really heavy right now, and I think the most important thing for me to do is to fix my inside before I fix my outside. No one needs to tell us about the importance of weight loss – we get it – but actually it's never really going to work if all we think about ourselves is we're pieces of shit.

Any true medical professional who is worth their qualification in medicine should understand the long-term mental impact of shaming people for not being within their BMI. I understand it must be frustrating to treat patients if they aren't at their healthiest, but the truth of it is the more we make people feel shit about themselves, the less likely they are to access the correct help or support to get better.

It doesn't take much to realise that if someone feels shit about themselves and then someone confirms the shit feeling, it'll have a long-term impact on that person. Not only are they thinking it about themselves, they are also having it confirmed by someone else. It is the least helpful thing you could do and it could then have the effect of making someone become bulimic or anorexic, which is the opposite of making someone healthy.

I could make this an entire book. I could write forever about how self-care and self-esteem are linked to every single waking moment of our day and how we very commonly disregard them as something less important than they are. We can't deny the fact the things I have talked about in this book are everyday issues for many women. We struggle to believe in ourselves because the fear is if women were to truly understand their worth, men would be fucked because we would basically call for world domination.

But I can't go on forever, so here are a few key points I hope you take away from this chapter:

We are allowed to love ourselves endlessly, kindly and gently. We are allowed to speak to ourselves with softness and warmth, like we are nurturing the small child that we keep locked inside.

We don't need to shame ourselves for how we look, or what we haven't yet achieved.

This isn't something we can instantly fix; it's something that grows and it's something we must spend every day promising to work on a little more.

And finally, the most damaging thing that can happen in life is when we forget to believe in ourselves and pin all our happiness onto someone else's success or worth. We don't have to end up at the bottom of the pile, but the choice to put ourselves first doesn't come from someone else – it has to come from you. If you leave it to another person to prioritise your emotional needs, you'll dangerously be giving away the best thing you have, which is your own love and protection.

QUICK TIPS ON SOOTHING YOUR SHIT

All of the below things are the shit I do, sometimes on a daily basis, to calm myself. They have been stress-tested by *moi*, AKA me, and I can categorically confirm these things work. Guess what, though? Until you give them a go, you have absolutely no bloody idea if they're going to work for you. So, give one, two or all of them a go and figure out your groove, hunny.

- Breathe – it's gonna be okay, babes. Remember: in through the nose, hold it for a second and slowly breathe back out through your mouth. You're cooling your nervous system. Give your nervous system a piña colada and a moment to chill.
- Go outside. Even if you're sat in the rain, with a coat, breathing the shit out of your life, do it, because that fresh air is actually really important. Don't get me wrong, it won't fucking fix life, but it is going to give you a focus.
- What can you see? Is it the same four walls as yesterday? Then move! Move, baby girl. Move your arse real slow.

- Have you ever spent a hot minute to see how many colours are in a room? How many colours of green can you see? Count them!!

- Every step you take – I'll be counting you! Walk, even if it's upstairs or to the toilet. Count how many steps it takes to get there. Every time you forget where you got to . . . guess what?! You have to start again. Keep on pushing and try to beat your highest score (FYI: this isn't some random shit I just googled. I genuinely do this).

- Find something you love! I mean, you! YYYOOUUUU love. Not the fucking kids, not your husband, girlfriends, friend or mum! You. What is it? What do you like? What makes you feel happy? Colouring in? Plaiting a Barbie's hair? Doing lunges until you piss yourself? Masturbating? Whatever it is, do it more and know you're allowed it.

- Brain farts – get a piece of paper and fart out every single irrational thing you think is too consuming at the moment. Lots of people might call that journalling but where is the fun in that? I fart on paper daily. Will it take it all away? Well, we've established that talking or accepting the things that feel too much won't take it away but it bloody well helps. (Just to make it abundantly clear, don't literally fart on paper. Use a pen, but, ultimately, if farting on paper helps, who am I to judge?!)

- Positive affirmations are some of the most powerful things you can float around in your mind. The idea that there is no point to them doesn't make any sense, because all you end up doing instead is recycling the same really negative chat about yourself and how you aren't good enough. If you are able to believe the bad voices in your head, you are just as capable of believing the good voices too.

- What can you feel around you? Is it soft? Rough? Slippery? Warm? I am not starting the scenes of a porno here; what I am saying is that focusing on the everyday items around your house, which I would like to add is FREE, will help your mind to focus on something other than the depths of despair that you might be feeling at this moment.

- Meditate – easy to type and yet this is actually really hard to do. I have found it exceptionally hard, so I say this with a caveat and that is, if it doesn't work for you, please for the love of fuck do not beat yourself up for it. I have found Rebecca Dennis – the founder of Breathing Tree and author of *And Breathe: The Complete Guide to Conscious Breathing for Health and Happiness* – so helpful in helping me to find space and more kindness for myself. Her podcast and mindfulness sessions can be found across most platforms and are the only form of guided meditation I use. There are so many apps like Headspace, which are also so helpful to many people. I just never found they worked that well for me. It is also worth considering that trauma patients can find things like meditation incredibly difficult to do. So if you don't manage it, don't sweat it. While it takes practice, the point of any mindfulness is to soothe you, so if it's causing you too much stress, it really isn't worth the upset (in my very humble opinion).

- 5, 4, 3, 2, 1 – find five things you can see, four things you can feel, three things you can hear, two things you can smell and one thing you can taste. Now, I find this whole process pretty fucking stressful when my mind is in a state of panic, so I go with it and I just find things and feelings as they come. No order, just *There is a bird, I can hear the wind, I can see a tree, I can smell the dog shit that is on my shoe*. You know, don't make it a stressful thing.

- Communicate with someone. It doesn't need to be deep, or lengthy, just don't shut the door to others. It makes it so much harder to open up the longer you sit in silence because it only gives you more reason to believe no one will understand.

Now, my challenge for you is to go figure out what any of that means to you. Did it work? Has any of it helped? Did you give it a go? How far did you get before you gave up and thought, *This is useless*? Yeah, I know, I thought that a lot too. Hence why I have a back catalogue of things I now do, which help in different ways. The wonderful thing about finding your own strategy is if it works, who gives a shit!! Really, it doesn't fucking matter.

Lastly – you can do this.

CHAPTER 6

Therapy

Right, let me have a crack at this one???

Therapy. It saved my life.

The end.

Kidding, that would be an utterly shit chapter.

It is the truth, though; therapy has saved my life. It has brought a level of relief to me to be given the correct diagnosis of what I actually suffer with: PTSD. The definition of PTSD – post-traumatic stress disorder – is pretty broad; I mean, that can really show up in so many ways, but mine mainly comes down to being triggered (my favourite word) by panic and crippling anxiety.

Up until I entered into therapy – which is an experience I now joke about with my friends, telling them that my therapist is the love of my life – I genuinely believed I had maybe undiagnosed bipolar or multiple personality disorder (which I appreciate isn't actually a clinical term used any more) because before therapy all

I had to go on were these really overwhelming feelings of fear and anxiety. The highs and lows of my emotions. I am not attempting to make this a joke, although I appreciate it could be seen that way, but I felt so totally out of control when the negative chinwag of my wanker brain kicked in with self-deprecating bullshit that I gave that other voice telling me I was worthless a whole identity: Patricia, the unknown version of myself that only comes out when I sleep. (Just for the record, Patricia is not a real person; she's just the person who lived inside me, intent on ruining every single part of my life with her negative chitchat.)

It took weeks for my fully qualified psychologist, who specialises in childhood trauma, to get me to truly believe I didn't have something more serious wrong with me. It took her months for me to truly trust her.

I have skipped the part where I tell you about what therapy is and gone right into why I have an unhealthy attachment to my psychologist – who, as I type this, could potentially no longer be my therapist any more. As in, by the time this book is released, I could well have managed to find a place where I am no longer needing to see her. I say all this with a heavy heart because I feel attached to her in a way I didn't think was possible – it's called transference or therapeutic love . . . I'll get on to that later. There is a part of me that doesn't want to even suggest the idea that she won't be my therapist in the future because I am DESPERATE for her to be in my life forever.

She is, in fact, a connection through a friend. Kind of . . . A very close friend of mine is a psychologist. She has spouted quite a lot of brain-related facts at me over the years. Sometimes I've not paid it enough attention and yet in the midst of my panics during the early days of my shitshow, she was video-calling me and talking me down. She was calmly explaining how everything I was experiencing was fixable, and that I would get through it. It was the most excruciating period of my life where I just desperately needed to believe it; I needed to see how I could be over something so mentally and physically painful. She was on this Facebook page where all the cool cats and kittens hang that have psych degrees and she said she would ask for recommendations of therapists. Bada bing bada boom, in comes the LLOOVVEEEE of my life . . . *coughs awkwardly* . . . I mean my psychologist. To be completely clear, if it hadn't been for my fucking fabulous friend helping me to navigate this, I wouldn't have had a hope in fucking hell of finding the perfect person for my needs. I don't wish to put a downer on your Debbies right here, but I also don't want to take full credit for finding someone who I would probably marry in a fucking heartbeat because she has completely helped me save my own life.

Before I get into how amazing therapy can be, first let me say this: you can be a paying punter looking for answers with the best of intentions, and you can still end up with a shit therapy experience, giving your money to someone who lacks the real qualifications to deal with whatever you might need help for.

How do I know all of this? Because I have had said shit private counselling by someone who truly wasn't qualified. I have always, historically, been catastrophic at spending money on myself. I have always felt like I didn't need a given thing, whether it be shoes, or a chocolate bar . . . (wait, who the fuck am I kidding? I definitely buy myself plenty of chocolate). Well, I can add therapy to that list too.

When I was at my all-time rock bottom with my doctor's surgery up my arse about why I needed to start therapy, and little to no real understanding of what I should be looking for, I just googled therapy in my area. Good old Google! I then scrolled down and ashamedly chose the cheapest person on the list. I booked her, cancelled her due to my minor hospital admission where I threatened to kill myself and then rebooked her when the A&E department said you really need to keep this appointment, feeling like utter shit or not. So, I had my session, and I still felt like shit. I guess that was to be expected. I would yo-yo through each session, going from feeling so good, to then having this overwhelming feeling of 'I don't trust you'. I can't tell you why, she never gave me a reason to not trust her, but I would tell her openly that I was wondering if I was in the right therapy ('Because I really feel like shit,' I said, 'and I don't think I am getting anywhere').

I started to feel really panicked about life, about leaving the house, about even coming down from upstairs. I would feel terrified it was the wrong thing to do. I had no personal perspective on what my limitations were each day. I wasn't really being given any tools to manage all the shit that was being unpacked from my past other than to just 'breathe . . . and imagine a time when you were a child and take yourself there to feel protected . . .' which, when you have unresolved trauma regarding your childhood like I do, really didn't help. It didn't make me calm, it didn't help and it most definitely didn't keep me grounded.

When people would talk about strategies, or tools, I would imagine this place you went to in your head where you felt safe and which instantly took away all the pain or fear. Like, POOF, and now your pain is gone. Now, I know it doesn't work like that but as someone completely ignorant to this whole 'be at one with yourself' bullshit, I really was struggling with the idea of what a strategy even looked like. I wanted to see it, understand it. I wanted it to be really clear. It wasn't, and using one that made me go back to a time where I probably felt most vulnerable wasn't helpful either.

So, due to my overall distrust of the medical profession for pushing me to one side and for that terrible counselling, by the time my now psychologist came along, I really struggled to completely allow myself to trust her. What if she hurt me like the others? What if she said I was a freak? What if she called social services? What if she confirmed the fact I am beyond repair? I can only describe myself as a scared wild dog, backed into a corner, eyes wildly darting everywhere, wondering, *Who is going to hurt me and who is going to help?*

I don't want to cast any shade on therapists in any way, but underqualified therapists offering their services to people are causing long-term damage every day without realising it. That isn't their intention – obviously they are naturally caring people for wanting to even consider that as a profession – but there is no denying the fact that allowing someone to hand themselves over to you and trust you with their most painful past takes a lot of care and nurturing and you do need to really know your shit before you allow that person to do that.

At the beginning of this whole journey I had it in my head that I would be fixed in a month. The trauma and pain would be gone and I would finally live my life, having effectively handed over all my shit to someone else. I felt like I was failing when a month ticked by and I was still very much in the thick of it. I punished myself for not getting better quicker. Why was I still suffering? *I think other people heal faster from these things than I have,* I thought. *What is wrong with me? What am I getting wrong?* I look back at that Laura now, and I feel like she's a completely different person. She was so unforgiving and ruthless with herself, and she compared so much of herself, even down to how she thought, to someone else. She gave herself no praise, and no peace, which I think in turn only elongated the amount of suffering I felt because I wanted to be out of it sooner. If I had just accepted that moment rather than tried to wriggle free of it so much, I might have actually found peace sooner.

There are so many different kinds of therapy, and I am nowhere near qualified enough to even give you an insight into each one or tell you which one will work for you. I am going to give you the hard and shitty truth. The only person who can know that for sure is you. The other shit bit is you might need to kiss a couple of therapy frogs before you find your inner Princess Charming (this story doesn't need a prince). I found I needed something that would bring the most effective long-term solution and that actually allowed me to lay out my trauma. For me that was EMDR.

EMDR stands for eye movement desensitisation and reprocessing, which has been found to be highly effective in people who suffer with PTSD. Enter me, with all her baggage, saying, 'Hi, I heard you know someone who can help store all my shit for me.'

Basically the long and short of how it works is it will make you process all the unprocessed memories you have suppressed (mainly for your own survival) and allow you the opportunity to address those things: how they made you feel, all the emotions and thoughts that are locked up in those really fucking painful realities you have lived and probably never really spoken about. For me personally, the way I do it is I lift my hands across my shoulders like a butterfly, then use my hands to gently tap below my collarbone in a soft but fast motion, eyes closed, and I take myself back to a time that was effectively triggering as fuck. Cue all the snot, all the tears. I am then told to stop, take a breath and say whatever is coming up in that moment. Sometimes that could be a memory, sometimes that could be a feeling that goes with that memory. I found in the initial weeks and months that new memories would appear that I had never really connected to any feeling. I could have been doing the gardening and, PING, it would just kind of come over me. Like, *FUCK!! This connects to that gut-churning feeling I have had since forever, which is actually because of this incident that happened when I was 12 . . .* I was almost connecting dots I had never connected before, discovering what led me to hate certain things about myself. The wonder of this process is no one can tell you it's wrong because it's all about the beautiful coding of your brain. The memory and the feelings are yours, so no one can say they're wrong!

As you can imagine, having to go back to a time when I was sexually abused was no walk in the park, and I resisted it week after week, trying to find other reasons why I could have suffered with these breakdowns. My therapist said to me one week not too long into our session, 'Laura, you have just talked about feeling really unsafe and terrified of someone else hurting you. When else have you ever felt like this?' The answer was there, on the tip of my tongue, and I knew I had to say it because I was having to admit that a lot of the unresolved turds from my past just weren't loosening off and were fundamentally a very large part of my whole belief system. 'When I was sexually abused,' I replied, and I remember how it felt to say it. It felt so painful because I was already clinging to the absolute edge of my life by my fingertips; the thought of having to verbalise all the awful things I've lived through felt too much.

Thankfully for me, my psychologist really knows her shit, but I was still resisting the idea that I could trust her. What if she wasn't really qualified in anything? What if she didn't know what she was talking about? What if she actually wanted to make me worse, like all the other people? These were my thoughts; I couldn't trust anyone and yet she was all I had and she seemed to make a lot of sense. She also never seemed to take it personally when I fed all this paranoia back to her. Luckily!

In fact, the first time I met with her, it just felt weird, awkward and almost clumsy to tell her exactly what I was thinking, but I was so desperate that there just didn't seem to be any room for holding back. I just let her have both barrels while still having this feeling of *SHIT, don't say that!* I would sometimes say to her, 'I don't want to tell you this because you might think I'm a weirdo . . .' Because in therapy you end up talking about the things you wouldn't ever tell anyone – the horrible thoughts, the past experiences, the ways in which you might have punished yourself . . . And then when I'd tell her those things, she'd just take a breath and say, 'Well, you're going to have to do a lot more than that for me to think you're a weirdo.'

I think the bravest thing I have done in therapy is be honest. As the process has gone on, and I have found out how kick-ass my therapist is, I have realised I can tell her anything and she will not judge me for it. I can be open with her and she can help me understand it for myself. She doesn't put words in my mouth, she doesn't give me a reason to believe I am wrong and doesn't question what I am saying. She holds space for me to be brave and open, and honest about my experience, and she never invalidates it.

Thanks to Covid, I have never met her in person; I've had all my sessions via Zoom. Regardless of what people might say about that approach being maybe not as authentic, I'm just pleased she hasn't seen in close detail the amount of snot that hangs from my nose as I speak to her each week and bawl my eyes out over what a mess I feel my life is.

I don't have the counterbalance to compare whether I would have benefitted more from face-to-face sessions, so it really is impossible for me to work out which would work better. But I can't really fault this experience of doing it via Zoom.

Even though this experience of sitting in front of a camera each week might feel impersonal to some, the fact of the matter is my therapist still managed to be completely present, constantly validating me and my experience. That has been so incredibly important for me. I have expected at every turn for people to question my sanity, my ability and my history. I have relied upon everyone else's experiences to shape my own. I haven't been able to gauge how I feel without it being backed up by someone else: their reassurance, or opinion on something that belonged to me in my life. How could I expect that much from someone else? Therapy has taught me that everyone has their own version of events. You can't expect to change someone else's to fit your own purpose. They're entitled to see it their way, you weren't put in their lives to control how they recall an event. You should always just be there to nurture however that feels, and if you can't do that because

you are too close to the situation then that is also completely okay. Step away and allow them that space to
feel what they feel.

I have spent a large proportion of my life resisting
the temptation to feel because it comes unnaturally to
me to express emotions like sadness or anger. They all
seem like bad things to show. Actually, displaying those
emotions is a perfectly healthy way to live life. We are
all born with the full range of emotions and they are
there to be felt. They are there to be lived. Not like
how I lived my life – like an emotionless psychopath
who never expressed anything but calmness. I mean,
not that I was ever really that calm, but if I did cry, or
lose my shit, it felt completely out of control and
totally wrong.

Happiness all the time isn't possible; it's also exceptionally unhelpful to yourself and everyone around
you. The term 'sit with it' in therapy comes up a lot
and it's hard when you haven't learned to sit with it.
How do you sit with it? How do you learn?

I mean, fuck, I wish there was a straightforward
answer, but the only way I can describe it is by its
opposite: two years ago if I cried and felt pain I would
quickly stop myself and say, 'Pull yourself together,'
because that felt like a weakness. Strength felt like

someone who always smiled, no matter her pain, and who never expressed her true emotions.

If I lost my temper with the kids, I would condemn myself as a mother worthy of having her children removed by social services and I wouldn't stop punishing myself for it. Not just days later, but weeks, sometimes even years later. I never allowed myself to forget all the times I fucked up, or was a miserable bitch. I would play them over and over in my head most days. I didn't think I was allowed to accept them and let them go, because they were my cross to bear. I was to punish myself for the rest of my life while trying really hard to not get anything wrong again. Ever. The exhaustion of that is next-level real and actually so fucking unhealthy. I think some people might read that and it will resonate with them, mainly because I refuse to believe I am the only person who feels that level of resentment towards themselves.

Instead I am learning now to try and accept that all those things are okay. They happened and I made mistakes but I am learning from them because normal human beings are allowed to do that. We have permission to fuck up. Therapy has and still is teaching me to accept the fact life isn't perfect; it is really troubling and emotionally damaging and we all live with an inner child who needs to be soothed and comforted.

I want to continue to soothe the little girl that lives inside me (can't stress enough, not Patricia), who craves the tender touch of a gentle hug and an inner voice of reassurance that she did so well and how proud of her I am. I don't want to resist that part of me any more, because, when I speak to that inner part of my soul, I feel the warmth of its acceptance.

Therapy has been my lifeline in recovery. It has given me the tools to save myself, for once. No one helped me through this; no one can take credit for all the work I put into this, all the time, energy or money to save who I am. I know, and as heartbreaking as it is to admit that I wouldn't/won't survive another breakdown/ life haemorrhage/meltdown/mental health crisis, or whatever you want to call it, I know I can't do it again. I have believed multiple times that I'd reached rock bottom; I really like to fucking think this time was well and truly the bottom of the shit pit of my life. I can't begin to entertain the idea that I could or would have to get through it again because the truth is it feels way too hard to summon up any form of positive affirmation to explain how much I can't do it again.

I used to be of the opinion that when you find yourself in a hard place once, you know how to get out of it the next time. But now, I will never again think that inspirationally about something so utterly dark and horrible. I am now of the opinion you don't have to hit rock bottom to learn how to never get there. You don't have to have any form of horrific trauma to find yourself in therapy, clearing space in your head for better things and happier thoughts. I would say therapy is a basic form of self-care. I know I will spend the rest of my life in and out of therapy because I will definitely need to maintain that level of care, and I will have to continue to work on the things I have learned while being in it in the first place.

It doesn't have to be as deep as EMDR and I think I've made it really clear EMDR is deep. It's really intense; my psychologist often says I really didn't pick the easy option with regards to therapies. I am an impatient cunt; I don't want to wait for anything and I guess the lure of knowing I could unpack my shit-filled brain pipes quicker really did draw me in.

CBT (cognitive behavioural therapy) is commonly used within the NHS for many forms of mental health issues, but again, it isn't for everyone. I know a lot of people who've completed CBT, which is usually six sessions on the NHS, and said it really didn't do enough or anything at all. Well, more than likely it wasn't enough (more on that later) but it could also be that it just wasn't the right thing. Just because your doctor recommends it doesn't make it fucking gospel. Doesn't mean it will actually be for you! You are a unique individual who has so many needs and wants and expectations, and being referred to one person to automatically fulfil all of those won't always be achievable. That is completely okay! It doesn't make you wrong! Your treatment can be as simple as art therapy, or gardening, or yoga. It can be so many different things, but you have to make that conscious decision to show up to it and give yourself over to it. You can arrive as the pessimist who feels a bit like the person at a séance who doesn't believe in ghosts, but you have to go with the intention of giving yourself over to this thing that is going to change how you believe and live.

Why yoga? Because it's about bringing you to a place that feels calmer. It's a practice that doesn't judge you and also helps you to focus your mind on the movement of your body and not the whirling chaos of your mind. I think I feel yoga is forgiving, if that's even possible? It just allows you a space to feel strong, peaceful, powerful and mindful. You can lose all those feelings of being anything other than the person sat on that mat doing your downward dogs or yogi push-ups (which, by the way, I can't fucking do).

I can see now why and how people can go to a yoga retreat and find themselves naked dancing in the woods, high on their own serotonin – because they leaned into this idea that they are capable of their own love and strength. They realised they can just completely release themselves from the shackles of life and let the good times of being free in the moment flow. It isn't a place I am at personally with my yoga – I am yet to strip naked and minge-lunge through the forest – but something about it feels inviting because I have suffered so much at the hands of others, but also with my own hatred for myself, that I want to just completely let go and feel safe to do so.

Has therapy done that for me? I guess so, because it has freed up a lot of clutter that shrouded my brain. At no point am I suggesting you will become a yoga enthusiast if you do six sessions of CBT through italk, but I am suggesting that if you work on the things you've gone through and continue to accept yourself for who you are in this moment, it can bring a level of relief and make you dare to do something you might not have done otherwise.

I used to joke about aligning chakras and yet I am now that person who can find herself crying in the middle of yoga because my emotions have come to the surface for whatever reason and, in that moment, I am letting it take me on a journey that I no longer resist: the journey of healing, which sounds tacky as fuck and yet it is a really big thing I feel on a daily basis. I am healing; it's a bit like I've had open-heart surgery, only the scars can't be seen and the only long-term effect it has had are all the memories that hang around my brain like dusty cobwebs in your nan's bedroom.

In short, if hitting rock bottom had a Tripadvisor page, I would give it zero stars across the board. While I could come up with some beautiful anecdote about how hitting rock bottom teaches you so many beautiful things about your journey on the way up, I think the fact I am still spreadeagled between surviving my shit and being at rock bottom makes me categorically confirm there is nothing at the bottom you can't learn at the top. You do just have to be open to it.

Would I have learned as much about myself if I hadn't gone through this utterly bullshit transitional period in my life?? Absolutely not, and yet I can still say, like projectile spew, it's better if you can avoid a breakdown altogether. It's better to find ways to cope with your mental health, like going to therapy, before hitting rock bottom. In short, get that help sooner than I did! Will you one day wake up and go, 'Well, that's someone else's shit to deal with, now, HA, GOOD LUCK'? No, although there have been many moments in this process where I really have waited for that to happen. Imagine my disappointment when I've woken up each morning wondering why the fuck I am not fixed, with a great pair of tits, a mansion and a vagina that doesn't look like it was repeatedly fisted by the Hulk in the dark. We aren't going to just wake up and find it's all disappeared; we are just going to slowly wake up to the realisation that our past doesn't have to represent our present or future. No matter how torrential the rain of our past feels beating down on our old beaten bones, it is gone now. We can learn to slowly let it go, and let it be there, gone but not forgotten.

I hilariously emailed my psychologist after she had been off a week poorly saying I was so thankful she was okay, that I had missed her and that I had catastrophically imagined it was far worse than what it actually was and worried she might have died. She replied saying, 'I will see you next week, Laura; we still have much work to do.' So, to sum up, you are currently taking advice from a woman who is in therapy and has an unhealthy attachment to her therapist, so much so that I told her I was terrified she had died (probably from a cold) and I had missed her.

I have been told many times over that when my time in treatment comes to a close and therapy has served its course, I won't feel this level of attachment, and yet, fuck my life, I am pretty close to dedicating this book to her because I feel like she has saved my life more than anyone else has ever saved my life before. If that isn't a calling card to anyone on the fence about therapy, I honestly don't know what is.

I know some of you will read this book and think, *Yeah, but I CAN'T AFFORD therapy,* and I completely understand that. Most people on minimum wage, with mouths to feed and rent to pay, don't have the easy access to private therapy to discuss anything. That is why it is important and beneficial to access places like MIND or even italk and, yes, I hear your patronising laugh as you pat me on the head and say, 'Laura, the wait times for italk are 633 weeks long,' but what is stopping you from adding yourself to that list? Why are you making this decision to dismiss it because no one will see you immediately? Even me, the private paying patient, I still had to wait, and granted those

wait times were smaller but I didn't have a team of people arrive and whisk me away. I fucking wish they had,
but I think that is called rehab and is overall a lot more
expensive. Trust me, I know, because during one of my
many out-of-hand panic attacks, I googled rehabs to
see if I could afford one. I couldn't, and so I lay on the
sofa sobbing as Steve had to assure me no one could
care for me like he could and that I didn't need to leave
my house and go somewhere else to get better. He was
right, and yet at the time I needed attention and wanted
help there and then. Didn't really matter where I was,
no one was going to get that pain away.

So, I go back to my point: yes, our NHS is massively overrun, underfunded and disgustingly
overlooked, especially with regards to mental health
services, and yet my first question still remains: what is
stopping you from being added to the list and waiting?
The other thing I would urge you to do is find out
what community-based charities are in your local area
to help support those suffering with mental health
issues. My local area has a MIND charity service that
provides much shorter wait times than italk and provides CBT therapy. Again, I know this because I
signed up for it in the early days of 2021 and, when the
opportunity came up to start, I was already with my

said therapist and reluctantly gave up my place, because remember I was that whole 'I don't trust you' paranoid mess of a woman back then, who wasn't sure if said qualified lady was actually out to make me suffer . . . so I gave it up and that place would have gone to another deserving person who needed help.

The point is there are plenty of opportunities to heal; you can read the pages of books and follow accounts on Instagram that actually promote how healing can happen through yourself. I personally wouldn't have known the square root around my own arsehole to manage any form of self-healing without help, and yet there are many people who do.

I promised to talk about therapeutic love or transference. So, here is my take on it. There are very few times in your life when you feel completely vulnerable, I mean truly helpless, other than that time you are birthed from your mum with the world brand new and scary, and so you solely rely on that person to love you, care for you and guide you into childhood and beyond. I feel a bit like this is a perfect description for the love I feel for the only person who has ever sat and listened to and validated my experience: my therapist. You trust them with your life, you trust them with your story and you allow them a piece of your soul with the promise they will nurture and take care of it, rather than flatten and destroy it.

I have never told anyone everything that goes on in my head. I have been terrified someone wouldn't understand, that they would condemn me, shun me. So, along came this wonderful woman, who doesn't mean much at the beginning of the journey, and yet, as the process goes on, and you allow that person to know more of you where they don't bat an eyelid at whatever you might tell them, you find yourself completely encased in this level of trust. I am yet to work through my therapeutic love with my therapist. She has told me that time will come. I think I might have been the one who fell through the net and forgot the fact this woman helping me is a normal person and isn't God. I have put her on a pedestal (I'm good at that) and somewhere along the line I am going to have to admit and accept she pisses, shits and farts like the rest of us.

I don't know if this is a good way to explain what therapeutic transference feels like, but it basically means you trust this person with everything, which in turn means you get the absolute best result from ther-apy. You aren't fucking about with poor connections and struggling to completely dive off the board with what you want to say – you just say it. Whatever the fuck that might be – 'I imagined punching my brother in his sleep when I was six'; 'I sometimes think about sticking a knife in my eyeball even though I don't want to do it'; 'I think I am bisexual but no one else knows'. Whatever those things are, you are in a place where you can share them.

I appreciate I have spoken a lot about my adoration for my therapist and it might almost sound repetitive but I think it feels so important to me to stress how crucial that relationship is. Without this feeling of safety I wouldn't have given myself over to her like I did; even though a part of that was my desperation to feel better, there was also a large part that didn't feel danger around her. If you do not have that connection, therapy will be so much harder to manage. My previous, less than successful therapy had points where I would think, *But I told you this already,* and she had completely forgotten; she had taken no notes, nothing to remind her of what we had discussed. We're all human, I'm not judging her for forgetting, but the repetition of forgetting made me lose trust in her, made me question her. So, my reason for banging my drum about this relationship is because it is so hugely important.

As a survivor of abuse, it has been a hugely important thing that has helped me to recover and I didn't even realise how important that was until all of a sudden I was in the throes of this feeling that she was literally there to look out for me, get me better and set me on my way in life.

How the fuck can you do that as a therapist and manage to detach from those relationships? The very thought of it yanks so hard at my heartstrings I could cry. I can't imagine how you manage to effectively let go of so many people, bringing them in at their worst and waving them off at their best. Or better version of! I guess that's why they do what they do, and why they go to university to get those degrees; it also only shows how fucking amazing they are at their jobs.

So much is said about how four or six sessions should be sufficient to address your issues and learn techniques to serve you for the rest of your life. I mean, I get that I have basically been like a rickety old jigsaw for pretty much all of my life, plagued with so many horrible memories, but I truly have no clue how I could ever have managed to walk away from therapy in six sessions. Is that achievable? Is it doable? I think the thing to really focus on is the fact that six sessions will *help* – they will provide some assistance in giving you some clarity – but sadly our NHS is too massively underfunded to provide the adequate sessions for every person's needs. We might feel broken in our experiences, but so is our mental health system that doesn't recognise the need for more funding and resources.

I also accept the fact that I will be in and out of therapy for the rest of my life, because you don't just stop going to therapy because you've been fixed. I think I will at some point finish EMDR, and then at some point go back into another form of therapy again. I will need to do this because the brain will need a little moving around and that is actually really healthy.

Above all else, give it time and work with what you have. If all you are limited to is six sessions, don't believe you have no hope and there is no point. There will always be a point to learning new ways to be you and awesome. I feel braver now than I ever have. I have been told I am so brave for daring to bare my skin on the internet, that people wished they had my confidence. I think none of that came close to showing the level of bravery it has taken to just speak about these issues at this time.

I haven't swept them under the carpet, or tried to deny them any more, I have just tried to make good with what I have and been honest enough to hold my hands up and say, 'This is me.'

I sometimes wonder where I'd be now if I hadn't started this process. I can't even imagine the version of myself who didn't go to the lengths she did to not die. As dramatic as that sounds, it's the truth. I was fighting for a reason to live and not end everything. I was trying to find a solution to survive and trusted people enough when they said, 'This isn't the end, you will come through this.'

Wherever you are right now, whatever that journey looks like – if you have previously had therapy but feel you could do with it again, or if you haven't done it and feel too scared to try – I understand. I have been that person saying to my friend repeatedly, 'I know I need to go to therapy, but I am not ready yet; I am too scared.' Even though I wish I'd done it sooner, maybe if I had, I'd have not found my psychologist, maybe I'd have continued with the shit therapy, maybe I'd have given up when things got tough? I'll never know, but with the shrill ring of the past still echoing in my ears from that catastrophic event in my life, I can honestly say I am so thankful I just took the leap and did it; no matter how painful it felt, and how scary the unknown was, I just gave it my best shot.

You do deserve this; you are entitled to it and you are not broken.

CHAPTER 7

I Hate Men

'Men are afraid women will laugh at them.
Women are afraid men will kill them.'
Margaret Atwood

'Each time a woman stands up for herself,
without knowing it possibly, without claiming it,
she stands up for all women.'
Maya Angelou

You wake, it's early, and you slowly start to stir, feeling around in your blurry-eyed wonder for him in the bed, but he's not there. You uncoil with a wide stretch as you roll over and are suddenly aware he is leaning against the door, silently, patiently looking at you. Instantly you feel his eyes touching every inch of your body and he smirks; he knows what you want. His thick, broad muscles are flexed, and his chocolate-brown messy hair hangs heavily over his head. He drips with sex as you see his chest rise up and down deliberately hard, and, rasping, he says, 'Morning, sexy,' in his slow, deliberate deep voice. He takes both of his hands above his head, leans into the doorframe of the bedroom and bites his lip as he looks you up and down. 'Did you miss me?' he asks, as you ache for him between your legs. Every inch of his being is there as your servant, his intense desire to make you happy is intoxicating, your pleasure is his priority . . .

Sorry, ladies, halt your urge to touch your clit and smack one out. This dude isn't real. He is a fantasy. Truth is, men like this don't exist, but we like to believe men really are designed to treat us like equals, and how all the hot guys aren't modest or egomaniacs. I love a fantasy as much as the next horny woman; in fact, just writing this little bit about the fictional guy in my dreams turns me on. I am okay with that but I am very clear in understanding this man DOES NOT EXIST, which I think is forgotten all too often and all too quickly.

So, as a woman in her thirties holding down a rela-tionship with a man and also raising two boys who I carried and birthed from my own body, it really is quite the statement to say I hate men.

Luckily for them, I am rather fond of them and I would quite like to keep them. And yet the title still stands: I hate men. Mainly because, as I have mentioned a few times in this book, they take the piss a lot. They abuse their power, they swing their dicks around like we're all waiting for a sausage to the face, and they often completely overlook the strength of women.

Yes, of course there are the good guys of this world. I hear them, I see them, but frustratingly they aren't the men who, on the whole, run the companies, or are in power.

It's the men who feel they have a level of strength over women, or even society, who abuse their rights as penis owners. I have been sexually abused, I have been mentally abused, physically assaulted and threatened, all by . . . men. I have seen across newspapers and court documents and heard really ignorant people in the press say that when women have been assaulted it's their fault. They say that they wore provocative clothing, or that women who go out after dark are asking for trouble, or that men can't be expected to control themselves around women. That boils my piss! I have every right as a woman to walk out of my fucking house naked and stroll down the street if I want to, with no threat to my life or body, and yet that isn't the world we live in. Back when the Yorkshire Ripper was at large in the seventies and eighties in England, the answer to keeping women safe was effectively to tell them they had a curfew and they must stay at home. When more women were murdered, they were labelled as problematic for putting themselves in unnecessary danger.

They were considered bad mothers and they were branded with 'they got what they deserved' by the media. They knew the person behind these murders was a man – they at the very least had a fucking big hunch – and yet it was women who were expected to stay at home, not men. Men might have been the threat but they also weren't the problem; women were the problem for owning vaginas.

The reality of any assault, rape or abuse is the victim or survivor is left feeling like it was their fault. They live with the guilt of believing they asked for what they got. Our policing procedures are changing and yet they still aren't in the favour of the person who experienced the abuse. This isn't just women; it is men too. I'll say again, my issue is, by and large, with men but it is specifically with the ones who completely lack any form of care for other people. My issue is with narcissistic men who believe they have complete control. There is no denying that not all men are egotistical predators, but there is also no hiding from the fact there is a whole fucking big societal issue with how we allow men so much control that they are able to dictate our freedom as women, in the name of our safety.

We move forward to the now, well past the eighties and the Yorkshire Ripper, and you'll find the devastating story of Sarah Everard. She trusted Wayne Couzens as a serving police officer to take her home safely, only to never make it home. The fear she must have gone through is nothing short of devastating. But while there was an outpouring of sympathy for Sarah in the press, we once again saw the same shit pumped out about what women need to do to protect themselves from men, how it isn't safe to go out alone after dark and how to tackle a situation where you find yourself approached by a police officer.

We are told to walk with keys in our hands, we are told to tell relatives if we're going out, we're told we need to make sure we always check a police officer is genuine by calling 101 if they're alone and approaching you. Of course, the really fucking sadistic prick who wishes to kidnap a woman is going to happily allow you to make a quick phone call to 101.

What are we telling men? I get that it's important we make ourselves safe, but what as a society are we telling men? That basically they have zero responsibility to not rape, kidnap or murder women in sexually driven crimes because it is the woman's job to be safe. Why aren't we telling men to not rape? Why aren't we telling men that they shouldn't intimidate women so much that they feel the need to carry keys in their hands? Why do we sexualise stalkers in TV programmes? I know, I love Joe from *You* as much as every one of you reading this does. I hate myself for feeling drawn to an incredibly troubled male character, and I hate that I have this overwhelming desire to see him fix himself and no longer murder women while also getting away with his fucking mental crimes as he does. I know it's a Hollywood show, but the reality is stalkers aren't made up in Hollywood and they will go to extreme lengths to control, terrify and manipulate people.

Back in 2020, when women were gagging for excitement during the pandemic, Netflix released a movie, *365 Days*, that saw an incredibly rich Italian man kidnap a woman and mentally manipulate her until she fell in love with him. I remember being so excited to watch it based on the fact women were fanny-pumping over this guy. I started watching it and within minutes felt repulsed and uncomfortable by the fact he was so egotistical he thought shoving his bellend to the back of an air hostess's throat until her eyes watered was fun. I thought . . . *I'm sure it gets better?!* Well, take it from me, it didn't! My vagina was so dry, it had cotton mouth. I couldn't believe this man had been hero-worshipped. He was rich, fit, attractive and had a sexy voice. So all this pedalled was the fact men can do anything if they have enough money; they can literally fucking kidnap a woman and force her to like him, while no one bats an eyelid. It had a *Pretty Woman* vibe to it but the lead had an even bigger ego than Richard Gere.

Now, I love Richard Gere in *Pretty Woman* – no one wants him to show up outside my house in a limo with a bunch of roses more than I do – but if you have watched the movie recently you'll realise he actually really does treat Julia Roberts like shit to begin with. He treats her like he saw her – like a whore. Not a human, or a woman; he treated her like shit, and the idea that she could be passed around like a used paper bag among his cunt-headed workmates stings with the reality of how sex workers are treated.

It is just a movie, all these situations aren't real, they are an altered reality, but they also aren't too far from the truth. They show the bigger issue of how we absorb and look at the world. We all want to be swept off our feet by the rich man who washes away our problems with a wet sponge across our feet in a bath built for two. Have any of you ever had that experience? No! I imagine not, and yet we ache for it, so that's why we love the character of the lovable rogue who wants what he wants and goes to get it. That only further pushes this idea that men win, they rule and they call the shots. I am probably the most battered and bruised by men, and while I have lived with and felt the harsh tongue of many unhappy relationships I have had with women, I feel the most intimidated by men. I hate the idea that they are physically stronger than me and have on count-less occasions shown that in my life. It doesn't mean I have given up on men, or even feel all hope is lost, because it's not. There will always be hope, but sadly there will also be the challenge of the men who are raised to believe they are the alpha.

I have pushed the boundaries of being a woman and not wanting it to define me because I feel rage over the fact I need to be careful, all because I am a woman. I have gone out after dark to wait for the friend to collect me in her car because I feel enraged that I should have to sit inside my house to keep safe, but women are losing their lives daily, all because of the simple fact they left their home. Whatever reasons lie behind these sick and twisted crimes, I lack empathy and sympathy for the perpetrators, which I guess is why I would always make a shit therapist, because regardless of the reasons behind their misogynistic behaviour – whether it's because maybe their mum was a terrible person, or something awful happened to them as a child that led them to do terrible things – there is still the issue of 'But what did *she* do?' The victim, the survivor. What did she do? She simply left her home, she went to work, walked to her car, went for a run, or even, in some cases, just ended up living with that person, which meant not even her home was safe.

We glamorise violent men as rogues who need to be loved and cared for. I'm sure they do need those things, but why the fuck does that make us their emotional and physical punching bags? Why are we attracted to bad boys? I am! Even though Steve is the most vanilla man going, who is more likely to cry than fight when he drinks alcohol, it doesn't deflect from the fact I love watching and hearing the stories of bad men turned good. How often do we give women the opportunity to turn good? We don't! They are normally made a spectacle of and never allowed to forget whatever they did. The mistakes we make are the lessons we learn, but we are normally too quick to condemn a woman for all her mistakes. We tell men well done for trying their best, we coo over men who take their kids to the park alone and we idolise single dads. All because they are doing the job literally millions of women do with absolutely fuck all praise because it is, by all accounts, our job!

Men hold their hands up and say, 'I don't understand, why do you hate us so much? I've never done that before! I'm not this person.' Congratulations, but the issue isn't with your idea that you don't need to change because you've never raped or mistreated a woman. It comes down to the fact you believe the only job you have to do in life is not rape someone; it's actually about calling out toxic masculinity when you see it!

If you read that and say to yourself, 'Well, this isn't my job or problem', then it also isn't *my* job or problem as to why I detest men who think a woman's problem is just hers. If your wife or daughter was abused because of her gender, would you still feel so passive-aggressive about your responsibility to make sure men treat women with respect? I imagine it would be a fucking big priority all of a sudden and yet no woman or girl should ever face any form of abuse for that point to be proven.

Okay, I'll hold up my hands and say it – I don't hate men, although the above would strongly suggest otherwise; I hate the system and ideas boys are born into and raised by. I hate the fact that even my own children, who I have always tried to encourage to express their emotions, will fall for the idea boys don't cry. One of my very own children has told me that if he cries, he gets called names at school. So, while I'm here banging my drum and demanding a better opportunity for everyone, there still seems to be a bigger issue that I don't think we will ever completely tackle and that is what and how we define men.

We like them strong, emotionless (but not too emotionless), reliable (but not clingy), loving (but not smothering), hardworking (but making sure to make time for us at the same time) and giving. I find myself drawn to and disgusted at the same time by men who can own a room. I am drawn to their confidence and intrigued by how they command people, but I am disgusted by myself for being so easily excited by an ego that big. Even more so because when a woman does the exact same thing and brings the attention of a room to her, she is given very different names. Like man-eater, attention whore, easy, nasty, rude.

We do this a lot; I see it. I don't know if there is some kind of social experiment that has already happened where strangers react to the presence of a confident man versus a confident woman (if not, it should be performed) but I would put money on the fact the overall confidence and respect would more than likely fall in the man's favour.

This whole time I have lived believing the way I change the world is through my children and allowing them to believe they are enough the way they are as they arrive in whatever form. And yet they too were fucked from the moment they were born – much like women – because they also fall into a societal view of what a man should look and sound like, and how he should behave to be given the chance of success and love. Yes, my boys stand a much better chance of knowing how to cry once they have grown up, having been given a safe environment to allow those emotions at home, but how much will the world judge them for it? How often will they be ridiculed for their vulnerability? Will they find someone who nurtures their needs? Or demands the typical model of a man to give them the love they think they need?

The way we create safe environments for women is to educate not just ourselves, but the men we have around us too. It is impossibly difficult to cull the dick-heads and filter out the morons, but why aren't we allowed that? For our kids? For ourselves! Men, for the most part, run the world, and in some parts they literally do as they please, including having a party in the middle of a pandemic and labelling it a working lunch. That in itself is a complete abuse of power, as is the toxic behaviour of bosses who sexually assault their staff, movie producers who rape young actresses, and husbands who beat their wives.

I don't doubt all of the men who do these horrific things have a sad story that led them to this, but it isn't our job to forgive them for it. It isn't my job to try to understand why I have been mistreated by men, or to forgive them. I don't have to make sense of their reasons or justifications. I am allowed to not forgive and to hate them for what they have done to me, even if it is making me feel uncomfortable in my own body for being in the same breathing space as them. I am entitled to dislike them for that alone with no reason to explain beyond the fact they are fucking bastards for believing they had that kind of ownership over me.

According to UN Women, '736 million women – almost one in three – have been subjected to physical and/or sexual intimate partner violence, non-partner sexual violence, or both at least once in their life.'[1] But given that fewer than 40 per cent of women come forward to report crimes against them, I wonder if that one in three statistic doesn't actually come close to the real figure of how many women are subjected to violence.

How many women will read this book who have to some degree been sexually harassed, raped or abused, or been in a home with domestic violence? I am going to sadly say I highly doubt many women have managed to completely escape any of these during their lifetimes, whether in childhood, as happened to me, or later. It will always come back to the same reason, which is that men have always been given the power and women have always been told to accept it. We are taught not to speak up because it is normally met with questions over whether we are making it up.

Even down to the unasked-for ass grab from the guy at the bar; that is sexual assault but that behaviour has been so normalised that we wouldn't even pass this off as assault. Any form of unwanted attention or touch is assault.

I get there are stories of women who lie, which is infuriating because it only continues to fuel this idea

---

[1] https://www.unwomen.org/en/what-we-do/ending-violence-against-women/facts-and-figures

that women aren't telling the truth, which is massively pumped out by the press and media. They lynch any woman whether it be for having a court case over rape charges or sexual harassment. It was only in 2018 that a man in Ireland was acquitted of his rape charges after his lawyer pointed out that his victim was wearing lacy underwear beneath her clothes. So, for obvious reasons, that makes it completely okay for him to have raped her . . . FUCKING HELL.

So, the stat of one in three women probably doesn't even touch the surface of how many women have actually been subjected to sexual violence, because the system has historically been pitted against them in favour of men, who either believe they are entitled to do what they want or are so fucking mental they have the ability to lie their way through the crimes they *did* actually do with enough conviction to get away with it.

Questioning if someone is telling the truth, or even pressing them for more information they aren't willing to give yet, has a massively huge impact on the mental well-being of survivors of assault. It is giving them another reason to stay silent because why would anyone believe them? I have been completely overlooked by male doctors for my anxiety and mental health issues. I have needed them to help me, and no one has listened.

I have had one positive experience with a male doctor, who is the one currently dealing with my mental health and the only one that I could trust to get me the help I need. I am 37 years old and I can only think of one male doctor to have given me the treatment I deserved as a female suffering with mental health issues. That is devastating and it is one story of millions, where women have needed access to treatment they haven't been given because we have been accused of being hormonal (yup, that is actually something I've been told) or that it's all in our heads.

We continue to survive in this society where we aren't able to trust police officers, and there is no guarantee in the doctors, and we need to be mindful of what underwear we go out in under our clothes because the court system could undermine us for that too.

It's so hugely wrong and so how can any stat that represents women who have been traumatised by sexual harassment ever truly be close to the truth? How can any woman ever have safe passage through the field of whatever harrowing experience they have had without hitting boulders in the road and being completely frozen with fear to move forward? You can see how and why so many people don't move forward and continue the same loop of abuse or even neglect because they have stopped believing they are worth anything more. They somehow believe they deserve the abuse, that maybe it is their fault because no one reminded them, taught them or showed them why it's absolutely not okay to ever be treated like that. They simply stop believing they can survive without that person or that life. As ridiculous as that might sound to some, those trauma responses can kick in hard when they want you to believe you are never going to get better, that you'd better keep your mouth shut, that you need to just stay silent, because the overall fear is death or abandonment. You can't begin to imagine the mind of an abused person if you haven't been in that fucking horrific situation.

The state of the world we live in where women are the underdog is improving and yet I find that so fucking annoying because it shouldn't be a case of improvement. It should just be a simple case of accepting the fact women are equally as capable with voices that are allowed to be heard and stories that need to be shared without question or doubt.

An example of how indoctrinated into the patriarchy we are is how social media works. It is a very well-known fact that the vast majority of social media platforms are owned and run by white men – rich white men at that. The rules, the expectations and fundamentals of social media are such that no matter how much you believe you have control of your platform, whether it be private or public, you do not own it; they do and they have the power at the press of a button to remove you and all the things you have shared and the journey that has taken you on. I have had SO many fucking photos removed for either 'bullying and harassment' or for being sexually explicit. I can comfortably say this here because this is my book, but FUCK YOU. I'm the bully? I'm the woman selling her body for sex? I am an average-looking woman in her thirties who has had two children and is confident enough to share her raw experience of life and I use zero filters. I have seen across Instagram women literally wearing cheese wire across their labia and straddling the camera with their let-me-suck-you-off lips, and those images are never taken down for being sexually explicit, while they also peddle the same filtered expectations of what women should look like for men.

I, like many people across social media, receive hate on a daily basis. I have at times been consumed by some of the things that have been said about me because it is really hard to ignore them. I have reported those comments, private messages and accounts, only to be told they didn't breach community standards, but a photo of me in my underwear with my pants yanked up my crack can be taken down for sexual nudity. Okay, let's make sense of that?!!? We can't, and I imagine for the women who are trying to be braver, who are trying to show a little more skin and a little more truth, to then be silenced for breaching community standards in that way will no doubt give them the shitty feeling of believing their body isn't good enough, or sexy enough, and needs to be different to be considered acceptable.

Men are masturbating on a daily basis off the back of the shit kept up on social media. Don't get me wrong, there is nothing wrong with a cheeky little yank at the image of something you find sexy, but where is the line? When will it be fair? Why are bigger women with hairy vaginas and armpits still fighting to have the same voice and presence on social media without being automatically called a lesbian? Ugly! Gross! The only gross thing I find about our society is the fact we still see women growing something naturally on their body as wrong. How is it that showing belly rolls and cellulite is called brave? It's fucking NORMAL! Why and when did it become brave to show the things all women have? Oh, that's right! Because men from the dawning of time have controlled how we see women and so for hundreds of years (alright, don't fucking quote me on how many years) women haven't been allowed to be voluptuous for themselves. Back when Queen Elizabeth I was around, being hairy and buxom was alright. Liz was kicking back with her hairy vag, wooden whittled dildo, spreadeagled with a turkey leg hanging out of her mouth, and no one was asking her when she was going to do something about her waist size.

I see mega-celebrities completely naked, posed, airbrushed with not a fucking hair out of place never lose their images or voices; they have had facelifts and home gyms for much of their careers, and are crowned 'real' and down with what life is about, and I find myself screaming, 'REALLY????????? RRREEEAAAALL-LYYYYYYYY????????? Come on!'

This whole industry that we slurp up like a milkshake from McDonald's is created by men, it is managed by men, and the images you see selling reality are created by men for men. To live in the ideal of what a woman looks like, and sounds like, or feels like. This is all to benefit the pockets of men. That one image you see that stays, and crosses all the lines of social media, is a direct result of how men choose what is put out into the world and how they want women to be perceived.

We, generally speaking, shame the bodies of both men and women. I love a man with a six-pack; it must be the cavewoman in me that desires the hunter gatherer. I'm not saying there's no pressure on men to be pleasing on the eye because fuck knows I'm the first person to enjoy the visual delights of a buff man, but I also know there are plenty of men with their beer gut below their ball bags demanding their wives or girlfriends lose some weight because they don't find them attractive any more. How do I know this? Because I have spoken to MANY women who have been shamed by their own partners for the size of their hips, or waist, no doubt because of the bullshit that is literally pumped out of the arseholes of tabloids, magazines and social media like a gigantic fucking diarrhoea shit.

The gigantic shit on the faces of women across the land is that filters and photoshopping exist. It completely removes the reality of what laughter lines look like, hairy toes and spotty arses. I used to be too scared to wear a swimsuit because I was sure my bikini line was broken; I was so fucking sure something must be horribly wrong with my body because all models who wear swimsuits literally have no sign of any body hair, and here I was effectively dragging my knuckles along the ground like a fucking chimpanzee. There we have the unattainable, unrealistic, toxic poster girl of expectation. The reality is that men need to wake up, grow up and open their eyes to what life actually looks like. It doesn't look like this thing you think! We grow fucking HAIR, and even the people who look like they don't have belly rolls STILL HAVE BELLY ROLLS! Come on now, lads, let's behave ourselves and remember that precious lady in your life deserves a lot more than your damaging, shitty little comments. If you want a healthy relationship, you're not going to find it with the sports model version of women either if all you're ever going to grow to is the size of the fucking foreskin that hangs from your head.

I will probably always struggle with the relationship I have with men and I realise now how that has affected my marriage and friendships with men. Steve has always been labelled as patient, good and amazing while I have often been seen as erratic, unstable and not deserving of him. Maybe that is true? But I still get pissed off by the labels, all positive in favour of him and nothing in favour of me. It is kind of the same shit pumped out over and over again in different ways through families and friends.

We are all responsible for this change among women and men. I have found it hard to listen to men, which is an issue. I understand why, because I think, *How dare you tell me your struggle, I don't give a shit. I am the woman who has felt intimidated by you! I don't trust you! I have lived in fear because of you!* I find myself wanting to be more accepted by men by acting like one of the lads with the bants and jokes so I am not seen as a possible person to have sex with. I feel less threatened when I can take the piss and be one of the lads rather than actually being myself. I didn't notice it until recently and yet I find it really hard to be feminine or completely relaxed around the opposite sex because I am almost waiting for them to make me feel uncomfortable. As I write this chapter I can say it has pushed me to have an open conversation with Steve.

I guess this is a form of therapy for me so hopefully it will be for you too. Maybe it will even encourage you to have a more honest conversation with your partner.

Steve is the typical white man; the overall struggle in his life has been relatively low. He hasn't been subjected to racism, he hasn't been bullied to any excessive extent and he hasn't, for the most part, battled with his mental health.

Then, in the process of caring for me and our children in 2021, Steve found himself starting to undo; he started to struggle with the things he would have easily managed before. He has always boasted about the fact he is a logical thinker and will only ever deal with things as they arise. That has changed for him in recent times and the pressure of what is expected of him as a man has kicked him well and truly in the arse. It has left him questioning a lot about himself and I think it has really given him a reason to pause and say, 'Who the fuck am I?!? I am a husband, a dad, a friend, a son and brother, but who the fuck is Steve?' He has, for the first time in his life, struggled badly with his mental health. In his words, 'I am meant to be the strong one. How the fuck am I meant to hold everything together when I can't keep myself together?!'

It makes me sad, and it shocks me, because I didn't realise he saw himself as this person and yet it all makes sense. I keep falling apart and I lean on him to the most excessive point of needing him to calm me down from every single panic attack I have. His emotional well-being is put well and truly on the backburner because I am clearly the one in more need. He then goes to work, he is expected to paint on the smile, deal with customers and never show the emotions or the fact he is struggling. He isn't happy; he is snappy, he is tired, he is quiet and, like most men, it's like getting blood out of a fucking stone when trying to communicate. Why? Because men don't talk about their feelings. I was so shocked when Steve said, 'Because I feel like I'm failing if I admit I am not okay, if I say I struggled when you were ill.' He believed without even realising it that being a man meant being the strong, silent type.

Had I hoped or looked for that ideal? No, but maybe I was drawn to it. Why? Because that's how we see men: as the dependable ones. So, when all of a sudden they aren't capable of being that person and their pressure cooker starts to boil over, where the fuck does all that emotion, feeling and story behind that feeling go? How long do they push the lid down on it all before it pops off?

This isn't what I want for my children. How can we raise two boys in the hope of them openly expressing themselves with a dad who is emotionally closed off? All this time, all these years, I have lived with a man who has learned to just be quiet because it's not his time, place or entitlement to speak up. So, while I have always joked about Steve being so laid-back he may as well be lying down, I now realise this is how he survives. He never stops being this person who is all chill on the outside because that's the expectation we all have of him: to be the guy who shows up and doesn't react. The cool-as-a-cucumber exterior isn't actually the experience of what he lives on the inside. Did he realise any of that before he started actually talking about his feelings? Nope! He just thought, *This is what a man does to be a MAN*.

I feel sad, and angry, because while I sit here and make out I have this idea sorted in my head about how fucking life works and how we can change it, the clear issue is still very much an elephant in the room of my house. I mean, thank fuck Steve has opened up to me, I'm hoping it'll give him the space to grow and learn how to be less of a selective fucking mute and more of an overall rounded man – one who understands that taking care of his well-being is as important as looking after our kids because they are looking up to him, searching for guidance and learning by his example of how he cares for himself.

Nothing about this situation is easy; it is actually impossible, and maybe I was meant to round this chapter up with some light, fluffy solution, like 'Let's all ride unicorns, smoke weed and chill, man.' But it's not ever going to be like that; in some part of the world, within some industries, men will somehow still make more money than a woman does for the same job. Women will still not be safe in the streets at night (or even the day for that matter; men don't just wait for the dead of night to do awful, shitty things). We will forever fight this battle of power. It shouldn't be about power, it could be about equality, but will we ever make that much progress? When white men with rich daddies run this country and sit in the House of Lords? Nah, sadly I don't think we will, but the one thing that can change with immediate effect is who we put ourselves around and how we allow them to control who we are.

The process of me being in therapy has given me space to understand the fact I don't need Steve. I mean, obviously I need him, but it's evolved into a completely different way. Not like an 'I've got my clit stimulator so I never need a man again' kind of thing (although that is tempting). I mean I can be emotionally stable enough to know I can look after myself when things feel too much, and I don't need to heavily rely on anyone else to stabilise me. Twenty years into a relationship and I have finally learned I don't need Steve to stabilise my mood or make me feel calmer. The woman who started this chapter saying she hates men, who realised in the last 12 months how much she pinned her overall well-being to a man and relied on him for emotional survival. You can imagine how well that went down with me, can't you? When the penny dropped and I went, 'Well, fuck me! I FUCKING NEEDED HIM ALL ALONG!!' That's when I started to make changes so I wasn't relying on him for everything all the time.

This in turn has sadly had a huge impact on him, which is now another process he is having to deal with. Not only the loss of no longer having me effectively hanging from his tit for reassurance, but also having to find himself. He is a good man; not perfect – I mean, he can be a really moody cunt, even more so recently with his struggle to find his feet in this new relation-ship we are developing – but he is, on the whole, a good person. He has a warmth about him that makes children love him, makes adults listen to him and makes me want to throat-punch him every time he eats chocolate.

He is the man we want our kids to be: the one who isn't set in his ways, who is learning as he goes and who's open to new ideas of how to be less of a moody prick.

We will always be responsible for ourselves; it isn't your responsibility to change the bad boy because you saw it happen in Hollywood. It isn't our responsibility to be angry at the world because it is largely run by men. It is our responsibility to change what we put ourselves around, how we raise our children and the conversations we are having with the people around us. If you're in a relationship with a man who isn't open to conversation, I mean that shit happens more often than not and that could be due to a deep-rooted issue from childhood, or even the fucking patriarchy, but is that your job? Responsibility? No, your job is to find your own feet and, in the process, find the person you are meant to be. Is that future unknown? Fuck yes it is.

For the first time in our adult married life, I have really questioned where our relationship will end up. I have whipped off the rose-tinted glasses and seen the fact we are both in a massively transitional period of time in our lives and we have no idea where that'll lead us. In four years we might not be together, but one thing I hope is that we're happy. I don't want to write off the past experiences we had; the overall public opinion that we're strong as a couple. I want us to be happy now, stable now, and prepared to work now. I am hoping that, in finding himself, he will learn to accept and let go of the shame of what is expected of him as a man. I want him to just understand he is more than the things society sees in him. He needs to do those things for himself, because it'll make him a better person for himself, and not anyone else. That is the closest I can get to a man's perspective of what it is like to live in the fast pace of 2022. What we see, hear, read and absorb will shape us in how we think and behave, and how that looks very much depends on who we become. The kids, they're watching and learning how we deserve to be treated and how we should treat others. If you wouldn't want them to be in an unhappy relationship, why would you want that for yourself?

I am not throwing around the idea that you leave Darren tomorrow and find a council house with your kids' Spanish tutor (does anyone really live that life?), but I am saying the men we surround ourselves with, whether they be friends or partners, have a massive impact on who we are as people. We deserve to surround ourselves with people who respect us as women, and if we have to call our boundaries in to protect us from the cummy goo of a man's small dick being swung around, then do it.

Sexism at large isn't going to go away, the pay gap isn't going to change quickly, but the way we put ourselves around men, and how we allow them to control who we are and what we say, is all down to us. It is okay to call bullshit when you see it. It is okay to just push your own boundaries when you don't feel like they are being respected. We don't have to like and love them all, and we have to remember the perfect man doesn't exist.

FUN FACTS ABOUT WOMEN THAT MEN MIGHT NOT KNOW

Come on, let's just have a moment to celebrate some of the things men might not know. That doesn't make them arseholes, it doesn't mean the guy in your life is doomed; it's just the simple fact men and women are very different. That is okay, this is healthy! Well, I want to celebrate women even more with this little fact list.

Feel free to leave this chapter open for the man in your life to read:

- Women have a better sense of smell. Read it and weep, boys, because a study published in the science journal *PLOS One* found that women's brains have 50 per cent more neurons in their olfactory centres. Unfortunately that also means we can be much more severely impacted by your fucking farts.
- Childbirth absolutely isn't the same as being kicked in the balls. While you might counter-argue with the fact that I don't have balls to know this, unless your jiggly sacks of flesh have been

booted for 38 hours straight, don't come at us, telling us you know what real pain feels like.

- Housework isn't our job, and don't say you don't know how to work a washing machine because if you managed to learn how to wipe your own arse, I'm sure you can figure out how to turn a tiny knob around and press start . . .
- Our clit has twice as many nerve endings as your bellend. So pay it some attention.
- We will talk about the patriarchy. Stop being offended by it.
- Please don't say you babysit your children. It makes our bumhole cringe.
- Toxic masculinity exists whether you believe in it or not.
- The pay scale around the world is still in favour of men. Again, you don't have to like it, but it's the truth.
- Boys' clothes are given adjustable waistbands. Girls' clothes aren't. I mean, like, age two and up girls aren't allowed to have the option of adjusting their clothing. They just have to have the next size up bought for them . . . and so we have, from an increasingly young age, the beginnings of weight and size dysmorphia.

NO SHAME

- Only about 30 per cent of women climax through penetration alone. Eeekkk – raise your hands, girls: how many of you have faked it to make him feel good about sex?
- Misogyny continues to be trickled out of the mouths of men who deep down believe women are flawed, broken or weaker than them. It is the downfall of every generation of man because it will never fully dissipate, and even the simple fact that I have openly talked about challenging issues like misogyny in itself will mean men (and some women) will be offended. (Don't get that twisted; it doesn't mean you have to forgive him for the backhanded comments or the subconscious negative behaviours towards women.)
- We are better at talking – to be fair, I don't think that is new to anyone.
- We have a better memory, which is why we are fantastic at dredging up shit from the past in an argument.
- All women have rolls, even the super-toned darlings who work out every day. THEY ARE NORMAL.
- Stretch marks are unavoidable. Stop shaming us for them, they show growth.

I Hate Men

- Saggy boobs are as beautiful as perky ones. They also know how to have a good time, even if they can slap a bellybutton at the same time.
- Our breasts are like your pecs. Stop expecting us to cover them up because they're considered shameful, sexual or inappropriate.
- We do love a bit of foreplay.

Did this help? One more thing: it takes men on average 2.5 minutes to orgasm whereas it takes women more like 12 minutes. I'll say it again, ladies: find yourself a good sex toy and get to work with making sure that every time you find yourself in the sexy times, you are able to OOOOOOOOHHH get there too.

CHAPTER 8

The Elephant in the Room

I feel like this is a subject everyone can relate to; it doesn't matter if you're rich, poor or famous. Everyone has dealt with this gigantic fucking elephant in the room. Covid-19, the pandemic, the global standstill of life thanks to a fucking virus.

I can remember the first time I heard about Covid. It was January 2020 and we were on holiday. Steve, with his wealth of infinite wisdom and groundbreaking facts, said with a straight face, 'There's this killer bug going around China bringing people back from the dead and turning them into zombies.'

I'm not going to lie; even though that is the most fucking stupid thing for him to joke about, it scared me! I think I've watched way too many zombie movies for that kind of shit to not be slightly terrifying, and so, as coronavirus grew, I really did just push it away. I really, really didn't want to face up to the fact that life could change for us. I didn't want it to, and while

I made every excuse under the sun as to why I thought it wasn't a big deal, deep down it's because I was really fucking scared. I was scared for my children, I was scared for Steve, for me, and I just didn't know how to even process this kind of information. How?? HOW can we be dealing with this right now? We have smartphones, and cordless vibrators; like, this is well past the days of the Spanish flu or the plague.

The weeks ticked past and more of it appeared in the news; it was unavoidable in conversations and I still kept saying, 'NAH, it'll be fine.' We had, like, two cases, but then those two cases jumped to five. Still I thought this just wasn't going to happen around here. The news scared everyone shitless, and still continues to with its really provocative headlines. I was obsessed with watching the news right up until recently. I would look at so many different headlines to see what our current numbers looked like, I would read the articles and then I realised how much it was damaging me and my mental health.

I can remember when Ebola appeared; out of nowhere all of a sudden people in Africa were dying the most hideous death possible and I was checking the news hourly to make sure we were safe. I needed to know I wasn't going to fucking catch that bug. Then all of a sudden, it was contained. It was managed and thank fuck it didn't break out to any unmanageable level, I thought at the time. I mean, thank Jesus and his disciples on that one! This isn't some conspiracy theory, by the way; I just felt like, as the Covid cases rose, I had this unwavering faith in science that a vaccine would be made in two weeks and we'd all be saved. Like in the movies, right before the big actor gets it, they somehow manage to be saved. So, when my friends talked about it, I dismissed it really quickly. I would say, 'NAH, not a big deal, I think it'll be fine. I really don't see it getting too bad; look at Ebola.'

Then March 2020 came and we all went into lockdown. I believed that by Easter things would be easing and life would go back to normal. Quite frankly, how the fuck can McDonald's CLOSE?? It fucking shut. I mean, nothing says shit is bad quite like McDonald's closing its doors. I just kept waiting for Tom Cruise or Bruce Willis to arrive and sort all this shit out. I can really remember this sense of 'but it will be alright because it just has to be, right?!?' I don't think anyone was any more shocked than me when it just appeared to keep getting progressively worse.

At first, I found myself almost enjoying the fact I could unplug from life. I liked that I didn't have to see some people, that I had excuses to miss out on things

I probably didn't want to go to anyway. I had this perfect reason to just not do the life I didn't want to do. Right up until lockdown I was in London most weeks and getting home really late. I enjoyed the fact I didn't have to do that. It felt good and there was a part of me that thought, *Actually, I'll never get this time with my kids like this again. I just need to embrace it and love the fact I can be home for them.*

Yet, I still couldn't stop looking at the headlines, and worrying about the fact it was getting much closer than I had hoped. I didn't want to lose anyone I loved. I was aware that the roads had become emptier and emptier. Things looked different now; life felt different. No more planes in the sky, no more lollipop ladies crossing children to school. It was like a ghost town. Slowly that thing that felt good about this situation – the thing that appealed to the lazy part of me – started to change and it no longer felt like a relief to miss out on being around people. It just felt safer and more comfortable. It felt easier to be in this place where we just did our own thing and didn't have to answer to anyone else, especially with that thing at the back of my mind ticking: that fear of the unknown, the fear of serious illness being a massively real threat for all of us, especially those considered vulnerable.

It was terrifying, the thought of losing someone and not being with them; the fear of missing out on final goodbyes. I know many of you reading this will have lost someone to Covid.

Schools closed, businesses forced people to work from home, tummies became hungrier, we had to fucking homeschool, hospitals felt the strain, we clapped for frontline workers and bought more take-aways than ever before because we were either too fucking drained to cook or felt justified that it was helping the community. I even had bags of sweets delivered to my house and convinced myself it was for the greater good of the country that I ate the fucking lot.

To begin with, I really took this relaxed approach to homeschooling. I promised that I'd teach my kids the things I never had time to before. I said I would show them how to top up the oil in the car, we would make cakes, we would go on adventures. I did the whole Joe Wicks shit; I even took part while wearing a roll-neck jumper because that's how together I am with exercise. I recorded myself taking part and all I managed to do was record myself looking like I was being finger-blasted and on the verge of cumming, rather than exercising. I started with a snack tray; they both got money each morning that they could spend so they didn't constantly ask for food all the time. I wanted to teach them so many things.

You know what I did instead? I bought a swimming pool. That is what I did! I did, like, three days of being this Mary Poppins mum I thought I would love being and then I enjoyed staying in bed longer and completely fucked off all routines because I just didn't enjoy being with my children all the time. I just didn't! I saw so many posts about mums who nailed this whole homeschooling thing, with kids tracing shapes on the garden patio and everyone looking happy. My kids stood in the swimming pool, throwing things at me, begging me to go into the pool with them so they could basically twat me over the head with a blow-up pineapple. But I didn't want to, I just wanted to sit in the sun and be left alone. I needed them to just leave me the fuck alone, but they didn't! Dog walks became a chore and I felt myself exaggerating that social distance to show everyone who passed that I respected and followed the rules. It is beyond me why I felt like that was so important, now that I look back. I think everyone did that, though; this really cringe dance around the fact we needed to justify why we were out. 'Look, I have a dog . . .' Walking the dog, minding my own business, walking the dog, keeping my distance, making it clear I am following the rules as I walk the dog.

Same for the food shop. I am asthmatic so to start with I actually felt too scared to go to the shop; I didn't want to risk catching the virus and then fucking dying. But then I quickly became very bored of the company of my children and as soon as Steve got home from work I was gone. I went to the shop and I made it last. I remember buying a tub of ice cream and lying to the person on the till that it was for my parents because they were self-isolating and they were feeling so alone. A fucking tub of ice cream. I felt like that was a luxury item and actually it was a complete piss-take to not just say, 'Look, I've got two kids at home expecting pudding tonight so this is happening.' I was only allowed to buy three tins of my dog's food, which was three days of dinner. I remember staring at the lady at the checkout blankly as she confiscated the remaining ones I had and told me, 'You'll need to come back in three days to buy more.' *Wait, so I need to come back out again, in three days into this shop to buy three more tins*?? I could understand how in the wake of everyone buying out all the toilet roll, there needed to be rations. I could understand we weren't to be buying 40 litres of milk, but my fucking dog's food . . . really??

We lost a lot, we lost people, friends, parents, loved ones. Did I lose someone? No, I didn't, thankfully, but I lost myself. I think we all have in these last few years. We have all lost a life we won't ever get to live. Imagine what would have happened if the big C hadn't appeared and swept around the world at the rate it did. Where would we be now? What would we be doing? Granted, that question can be used for every single decision we ever make in life. We will never know the other life we could have lived if we hadn't made the choice we made, but this choice, this situation, has been worldwide and it has literally robbed us of people who should have lived longer, who actually didn't have a long-term condition that limited their life. It has taken young and old, healthy and ill people, and it's been devastating.

The worst part of that loss is the really crushing fear it has left in those still alive. What if I get it and don't make it? You know, there really is no answer to that question either. The likelihood is it'll all be fine, you'll feel like shit, but then you'll recover and you might even get it and have literally no symptoms. Who can really tell you which outcome you'll have, though? And so I can see why people who have a compromised immune system live in a state of terror over how they might recover from it.

We have all lived under this cloud for such a long time, and the worst part is it still hangs pretty heavy over us. We have no idea what is next and I think before, we had this kind of cocksure feeling of knowing the predictability of life. We had enough control over how we chose to live. We have literally had that stripped from us in the most recent of times, and I wonder if this generation of survivors will actually manage to get over the effects of Covid. I don't mean the people who live with the long-term after-effects of having Covid. I mean the mentality of it. During lockdown, when all we had were our four walls and a whole lot of social distancing in the supermarket for the things that were considered essential, I remember watching TV programmes where I'd see people touching, or even being near each other, and I'd think, *THEY'RE NOT ALLOWED TO DO THAT!* My brain was so programmed to keep my distance that it just wasn't used to seeing people in such proximity. The simple act of physical contact really did seem so alien and I found it so hard coming back out and knowing my social cues. It didn't feel natural any more to socialise; it felt weird and awkward, like being on a first date with someone you're not sure if you like or not.

Everything seemed mad and I think it truly has sent some people over the edge. A lot of people even now don't know how to integrate back into society because they are scared of whether life will accept them back in. Being a social recluse for such a long time changes the way you see life and how you behave. I have realised now that if I were ever to find myself in a prison and in solitary confinement, I would be the person who shits into her hand and smears it on the walls while talking to my pet ball and naming it Wilson. I don't cope well with being withdrawn from society and I don't think a lot of people do. I think we all need connection and communication. So, when that is taken away you are left with a lot of mental health challenges.

The worst part about those changes in our mental health is they are slow, so it isn't as easy to pinpoint because you don't just wake up one day and notice something different. It's much more gradual and the longer it takes to acknowledge that change, the longer it then takes to come back from it. How can we even have had the time to notice those things in the middle of a worldwide fucking crisis, not to mention all while Donald Trump was the President of the United States. I mean, how many fucking crises can one world take?!

Our NHS has been under such immense pressure to cope with Covid, but Covid isn't the only crisis everyday life sees. It's just one of many, and sadly, as our NHS is horrifically underfunded, it meant that the people who actually keep it going – the doctors, nurses and care workers – were literally worked into the ground. Cancer patients had their treatments delayed, operations were cancelled and the mental health crisis leapt through the roof.

I was one of those in crisis and I felt every inch of the time that no one had for me. Was it their fault? They are human at the end of the day, and I was on a long list of people who just needed more from them. I get it, and while I have had a long history of poor healthcare from SOME care professionals, I also get the fact that on this occasion, I was suffering with something everyone was suffering with and that was burnout. Everyone was praying or wishing for the day when things might feel a bit better, a little less draining or lonely, when people might actually just treat them a little better. But each day would come around and the shit either got worse or stayed the same.

I don't know how you can continue to care for others when you are being overworked and patronisingly clapped for on a Thursday with no pay rise and a family that equally needs your time and attention? I have so much respect for the doctors and nurses who just show up each day and deal with the onslaught of the NHS. They might have qualifications in care, or even a degree, but that doesn't make them superhuman! Doctors and nurses were having to do this job while still having the same fears we had. The difference was we were in the comfort of our own homes with a much reduced risk while they were having to look after people who had this virus, who were dying in front of them, and then having to deal with the grief of losing someone they wanted to save!

We wanted an end, but so did they. So *do* they! We all wanted to see a resolution and I think we grew tired and pissed pretty quickly when we didn't get the things we wanted; a bit like spoilt children really. We wanted to go to the pub or a restaurant, we wanted to see mates or family, so we felt more frustrated and we took that out on everyone. Domestic violence was on the up and during the main lockdown we saw videos of how to save women in dangerous situations. I kept wondering how that would help. Did we think abusers wouldn't watch these viral videos of code words or messages that promised to save women if they were ever stuck and had no way out? Asking for a special eyeliner was supposedly the answer, and yet sadly there were so many women who lost their lives purely because their partners were home more and so they were beaten more.

People took out their frustration, fear and hurt on anyone around them. Shop workers, nurses, doctors, even banking staff. Once a week, we gave a moment of thought to those who had to continue to work through the pandemic by clapping on our doorsteps because they were considered critical workers for keeping the economy going, but did everyone stop to think about the fact these people didn't want to be in work? Steve worked through the whole of the pandemic as a front-line worker and his job at times was so stressful, I thought he might have been the one to have a break-down. (Which he did, actually, I just beat him to it.) People wanted a pound of flesh because they were over giving a fuck about anyone but themselves.

The pandemic has left us all ruined emotionally, physically, mentally. Relationships have broken down, and at the same time many couples have had babies because they suddenly had a lot of time on their hands at home together. I clearly missed the bit where I wanted to have sex with my husband all the time in an apocalypse because I can honestly say touching his willy was way down on the list of priorities during any lockdown. We have lost a lot, not just in time and memories but for some the physical presence of someone they loved.

The impact is huge; so huge it's almost impossible to gauge. The way we will all get fucked for many years to come with the cost of living and taxes, thanks to our government. More families will lose incomes as companies fold under the sheer pressure of surviving this with nowhere near enough financial support. Children lost the right to an education because, like most, homeschooling became throwing a 2p in the back garden, telling them to find it and labelling it 'team building'.

I have seen more people experience breakdowns in recent months than I did in the thick of it back in 2020 or 2021. I think a lot of people are now hitting that wall they can't move past, no matter how hard they keep trying. They want to just say, 'This is it now! We are coming out the other side' – we all fucking hope – 'so why am I now feeling this really heavy, hard emotion of breaking when I don't want to?' I really think it's because the vast majority of us didn't want to face up to the here and now; we wanted to keep looking forward to something good that would happen because then we would feel better. The future came, the socialising happened, but that same feeling of dread or unhappiness just didn't shift like we had hoped. I don't know that really anyone has acknowledged or admitted to the fact life has been really hard. No one wants to just say, 'Actually, I found this really difficult', because it hurts too much and so we keep trying to move forward while the arse of that elephant in the room grows bigger until there's barely enough space for us to breathe around it.

We aren't very good at just owning our own shit. Like saying, 'This doesn't feel good', because we normally back up whatever we are going through with 'but someone else will have it worse'. True statement – there will always be someone worse off – but does that invalidate what you have gone through? No! You are allowed to just say, 'This is fucking awful and I don't like it.' You don't have to acknowledge or regard anyone else's feelings because of the fact they might have it worse.

It is completely okay to just admit this time has been exponentially shit. It was the gold standard of turds, and I am yet to meet anyone who said they enjoyed it. Who would? Yes, it brought us all together in that we thought of others and were more generous.

But then we all started drowning in it, and we held our breaths to wait to come up for air, but the problem is we're all still holding our breath.

When do we get to move on? Although things are better, are they great? Far from it! I want to go back to the me who was listening to Steve in Center Parcs talking about zombies and I want to tell that Laura to just give herself a break. I want to tell her to not try to homeschool the kids because no other mum is going to do it and everyone will be really struggling. I want to tell her that it's alright to go out on your own for a walk with the dog and that you don't have to enjoy being with your children all the time. I want to tell her to get into therapy sooner so she doesn't have the breakdown she always promised she'd never have again. I want to tell her above all else to not panic! I can't, though, and so I do live with a level of regret because I really did do such a poor job of caring for me. I don't know that I did a perfect job of caring for the kids all the time, but I most definitely did the very best I could; even if that never felt enough, I was still trying really hard to care for them and just didn't do it for myself.

I have described myself in recent times as being the house on fire: I am always able to get everyone else out before the flames become too much but I am yet to manage to get myself out alive, in the sense that I never have known how to save myself first to then save others. I think that is more than likely a big issue a lot of people are seeing now in themselves. How could we manage to care for our own mental health when we were so focused on caring for the jobs we were balancing, the kids we were teaching, the Zoom calls we were trying to keep up with, and the marriage we were trying to maintain before it all went BANG.

When will it be over? When will it be enough? How much more suffering? How many more lives will be lost to Covid? Not just because of the disease but because of the lifesaving treatments that are being delayed because of it? At what point do we shut the door and shut out the noise? I feel ready, more because I need to move on. I need to find my feet without the real fear of 'what if?'

I want to say you just think, *Fuck it,* and do it, but it's never going to be that straightforward. We have to make time now to find ourselves and see what this new world looks like post-Covid. Yes, it will be different and unfamiliar and that isn't something we generally cope well with. Remember, our brains above all else want to keep us safe and alive, so if they feel that change coming, they are going to push against it, so that's a case of trusting the process and leaning into it a little more with each step in the new direction we are wanting to go. Nothing and no one can guarantee the ending. We might find it ends up being a dead end and we have to turn back around, but isn't it more important we give it a try than sit here, frozen in fear of the future? I just want more, don't you? Can't we want the things we maybe hoped for before this shit happened? Can't we need and look forward to even more? I think we deserve it now more than ever before.

This comes from a more spiritual angle. I don't mean I think you should believe in Jesus by the end of this book, because I am not a religious person. Even after all I've been through, I still haven't found the calling of the Lord, but I have found the spirit or spark inside of me. I think we all have it and it's been dulled down dramatically. Anyone who was suffering with a mental health condition before 2020 will most definitely still be struggling with it now because this hasn't been a period in our lives where we have flourished. It has been a period of time in our lives where we have stopped and waited for the green light. Well, Boris won't wave a flag for you to find yourself, and waiting for the gold at the end of the rainbow probably hasn't really got any longevity in it either.

NO SHAME

This is our time; it is the time of self-discovery. If you feel like the worst part of you came to the surface because of Covid, then make sure it doesn't stay that way. If you're angry, or you feel like you can't be the happy person you used to be, maybe that's because that old person you used to be needed changing and this bit in the middle where you feel the injustice of life has caught up with you is now the time to figure out who you actually are. We all waited for the end of every lockdown to make us feel better, and we still felt like shit, so it's time we acknowledged the fact the Pinot at sunset on the decking wasn't enough to make you feel whole again. Did you ever feel whole? Or are you just on the cusp of finding out what the 'whole you' really looks like?

I have actually had Covid, and I am also triple jabbed. I am at the point in my life where I would even grow a second head if it meant I could carry on living. Some will believe that is blindly following like sheep, but I am okay with that. I chose to listen to science, and not YouTube, which I believe has been one of the biggest divides in recent times. I am okay with whatever anyone wants to believe, and I am cool about who you choose to listen to. I ask that you do the same; your reasons for not taking the vaccine aren't, quite frankly, anything to do with me; in my limited medical knowledge, it is you who chooses to potentially put yourself at risk. I don't pretend to know the different shit that makes up the vaccine and I don't wish to pretend to have done six years at uni to understand it. The volume of facts out there from people less than qualified means the internet can be dangerous water to swim in, even though I know people are just trying to inform themselves.

We all have a choice; I chose to have the vaccine, and, while my symptoms of Covid when I did have it were mild, I wouldn't have wanted to risk catching it and dying. Quite frankly, dying is quite low down on my hopes and dreams for the future generally. This is another thing that I struggle with when it comes to social media, because the words 'freedom of speech' get passed around so freely now, it almost opens up this idea people can literally say anything to anyone and it's allowed. Freedom of speech! It kind of waters down the reasons as to why freedom of speech is important. Freedom of speech is about issues that carry fact. These things labelled as facts continue to increase fear even when they don't need to. We all get absorbed by them and it's impossible to ignore them because, unless you live under a rock, you won't be able to avoid hearsay, gossip, newspapers and social media.

I am the first to talk about the power of social media and how much of a positive influence it has been. It has given me the opportunity to write these books. It has given me the chance to be funny for the internet. It has given me so many chances, and yet there is no denying the fact it is toxic as fuck. It really does ruin so many people's lives; it makes people feel inadequate. Covid has played a huge part in making this so much more magnified because people have spent so much more time on the internet. What else have we had to do? We've all been stuck indoors, bored shitless. So, we have sat and drunk in the sights and sounds of what was on offer. Some of it has enlightened us, some of it has triggered us, and while we are completely responsible for what we consume, sometimes it has been unavoidable.

I love and loathe the power social media has over us because the more we are in it the harder it is sometimes to look up and realise it's not reality. The filters, the picture-perfect families and happy marriages we see completely plastered over it, the dieting, the skin with no sag or stretch marks. It's all so unattainable and it's all so miserable when the lines are blurred and we forget the fact it doesn't represent life. I have fallen victim to this perception in Covid and that most definitely went some of the way into explaining why I did have my breakdown. While it wasn't the main reason, and was far from it, it most definitely was one of the catalysts pushing me towards it. How could I feel so unhappy while everyone else seemed to be enjoying life? That's how it all seemed, that even those who were struggling weren't struggling that much.

I can't say I was completely honest with how I was feeling either because I felt like I just needed to be funny all the time, when in fact I just needed to be real; that's what I deserved for myself and all the people who loyally supported me too. They needed that truth and I was only able to give that truth once everything came crashing down to the ground.

We will never get this time back, and it hurts because we all understand the magnitude of how we only get one life and all that shit. We don't want to have kissed goodbye to two years of our lives. We have been promised freedom so many times, that the vaccine would change things – and it has, it truly has stopped this from killing more people – and yet there is no denying the fact we are all still living like we're walking on eggshells. The constant threat of lockdown looms over us as newspapers speculate on things they literally have no idea about. That then fuels the assumptions and gossip. All based on no facts.

No one can give us a glimpse into the future and I think it's something most of us would like more than ever because we just need to know whether we can get back all the things we lost. I fucking hope so! Time is gone and there is no reliving it, but the things we've learned in that space have been something we can carry forward.

I used to say before Covid that if I ever needed to homeschool my children I would do it. I now realise that I, in fact, am not in the position to lend my very limited education to my children to teach them the things schools provide on a daily basis, not to mention the fact I don't enjoy being around them 24/7. I can say I wouldn't have learned this if I hadn't experienced a pandemic. I would have much rather learned this lesson in other, less harsh ways, but it's a lesson nonetheless.

I have also learned how to breathe. Just breathe. That's it, you're doing it right now! You're breathing and I bet as you read this sentence you are very aware of how your chest is moving and maybe you can even hear the noise as you breathe in and out of your nose or mouth. See, you already nailed that one and you didn't even need to learn any lessons to ace it. I think it's just more about making sure you acknowledge that breath a little more in your life and worry a little less about the things swimming around your head in any one given moment.

I have learned to declutter my house and, while that skill could be learned at any time, the pandemic has forced me to be in a space where I was made to question why I have got all this shit. All these things I label as memories, for who?? For my kids to eventually have to deal with one day, once I'm dead? I don't think they give a shit about the table decorations I had on my wedding day, or the old letters I kept from school. When will I really give a shit to read it all? Look through it all? When will my children want all the cards they ever got from every single person in their life in that moment? I honestly don't think they will ever give a shit. So, I have let go of a lot of useless shit that meant nothing, as it turns out, not even to me. I was hoarding it because I thought I needed it to keep the memories.

I have realised I like my own space, and that's a good thing. I don't need anyone, literally anyone, to feel safe or capable any more. I can be all of those things for myself. I can enjoy the space and silence of being alone and not feel guilty for it.

I have realised I don't need to please everyone; that includes people on the internet, and, if I don't want to be on it for a day, that's okay. I can be a good person and look after myself.

Stop, give yourself a minute. Grab a pen and write down all the things you have learned about yourself in this period of time. It might look ugly, it might be that you realised you didn't love your husband, that you wished you had a different career. There is a lesson in literally anything we go through and some of those lessons are hard. Just appreciate the fact that, no matter how utterly relentless Shit-vid has been, it has taught us all something. You can wish to have had your time differently; that's something I yo-yo between a lot because I never wanted to go through what I went through, but I am forced to accept the fact I have gone through it and that I am a different person for it.

It's all a learning curve and sometimes I wonder how much of the curve I am meant to be on before the learning becomes clear. You are so much stronger than you even realise for having gone through something like this and still managed to pull yourself through. How many times do you need to hear that you did it before you believe you did it? Remember, none of those 'but someone else had it harder' thoughts; just accept and validate the fact you did it even though it all felt really hard and impossible. You still did it and so, no, we have no idea what is next or what to expect, which is hard for everyone, but you have managed to get this far. You did it even with all the odds stacked against you. All the times when you felt like giving up, you didn't. You kept on giving it a go, this thing called life. You just kept on, and so regardless of how monotonous day-to-day life feels, or how brain-numbing your inner thoughts are, you are still somehow, from somewhere, managing to pull it out of your arse. Well done, bravo and congratulations for facing all the hurt, fear, shame, pain and even regret, and still being here and moving on. Even if it's at the same pace as a snail, who cares? You are moving.

CHAPTER 9

You

In among all of this, is you. The person left reading this, or even me writing this. It all comes down to who we are and how we manage life. None of this balance is easy. It is challenging and it is draining as fuck. Our mental health and our journey through life makes up huge proportions of who we are as people and how we survive. Our overall purpose in life is about survival, and sometimes that can get lost when we feel totally consumed by whatever it is we are feeling or experiencing in a given moment, whether it's the ending of a relationship, suffering from crippling anxiety or even losing someone you love.

We are all faced with these things at some point in our lives and, instead of accepting that, we push them away in the hope one day they'll just disappear. My experience is that these hurtful things don't go away; they just sit in the background and wait for their time to be heard. Sometimes if we leave all those painful things to back up like a shitty clogged toilet, eventually the shit will end up around your feet and the smell will become so consuming that you can't pretend to not notice it any more.

Our brain is so precious, and it can feel like our biggest enemy at times. I have really struggled with this in recent years. Why? Why do I hate myself that much that I could think such horrible things? Or wish for myself to be dead. How could I want that for myself? The truth was my little old ticker had well and truly spent all its fucks holding itself up while I did nothing to try to care for it. I did nothing to care for myself at all. I had believed I knew what it was like to be strong, which really meant never being vulnerable, that ignoring my own needs to fit other people's was far more important than helping myself. At some point or another, the human body will say enough is enough when it is no longer being cared for the way it needs to be.

That might be personal space, a walk alone, going out for dinner . . . whatever the fuck that looks like for you, it is essential. The hardest part about it is finding out what it is YOU need. Have you ever asked yourself that? Have you ever given yourself the space to contemplate what you actually need? What brings YOU happiness? Because it wasn't that long ago for me where I sat there completely frozen with the nasty, shitty reality that I had no idea what made me happy. I knew how to make others happy, which in turn made me happy, but that doesn't have the same longevity as selfishly and rightfully spending time working out what Laura loved and enjoyed.

I have learned a lot about *me* in the last 18 months. I have learned a lot about trauma responses, I have learned so much about my reactions and how and why I have them. All those things have gone into my self-care strategy. I have needed those things to look after myself better, so that when those really fucking scary out-of-body moments happen, I can soothe myself. I can promise myself that everything will be okay.

I have learned that the different states of trauma responses are emotional reactions to trauma. That could be anything in your life and can happen at any time for any reason. Everyone's response to something traumatic is unique and should never be discredited because someone else experiences it differently. They are made up of flight, fight, freeze and fawn.

Flight:

- Workaholic
- Over-thinker
- Anxiety, panic, OCD

- Difficulty sitting still
- Perfectionist

Fight:

- Angry
- Controlling
- Bullyish behaviour
- Narcissistic
- Unpredictable behaviour

Freeze:

- Can't make decisions
- Stuck
- Disassociation
- Isolating

Fawn:

- People-pleaser
- Lack of identity
- No boundaries
- Overwhelmed
- Co-dependent

I didn't realise that fawn was even a thing other than Bambi. I have been fawning the fuck out of my life and thought it just made up who I was and that it was in my DNA to want to please people and find it impossible to have my own boundaries. How could I have lived my entire life believing that I needed someone else to survive when all I ever really needed was myself?

The word 'disassociation' hasn't ever really made sense to me. What does it even mean? It sounds like a fucking boardgame from the eighties. I realise now through reading up on it, I have very much disassociated myself from a lot of my life. I have sat and removed myself from situations I clearly didn't want to be in. I have simply gone into my head. I have felt like I am somewhere else. I have recalled memories with no emotion attached to them. I have pretty much recalled all situations I have been in as if looking at them from the third person, like I was a passer-by watching them from someone else's perspective. Like the memory wasn't actually happening to me; it was happening to someone else, but I was the someone else. I know, sounds mental, doesn't it? Disassociation is common in survivors of abuse, but for anyone who hasn't dealt with it, I appreciate it might be quite hard to wrap your head around. So if you're reading this and feeling complete relief that you've never experienced disassociation, don't worry, I understand because I have now seen the other side. I have noticed since having therapy that I am able to recall memories on a more first-hand basis and I am in my body, and there are feelings rather than numbness. I can recall a memory of something and know it felt good, or sad, or unhappy. It doesn't just feel like nothing any more.

Disassociation is having an out-of-body experience; feeling like you're not you, almost like you're someone else, feeling emotionally numb or detached, or possibly not even feeling pain, just feeling numb.

Those feelings, they're not your fault. They are your brain doing its very best at keeping you alive. Bravo to your excellent brain for being such a fucking hero. Even though it might not always choose the best course of action, let's give it a round of applause for always trying its best.

Our brains are complex, they are vulnerable, and they don't want to hurt you; they just need you to be okay.

I just needed me! You just need you! But we aren't very good at recognising that in ourselves at all. I have discredited myself so many times for my reason for living, or for being successful due to the people I had around me, I never gave myself any credit for still being here. Sure, having a husband who supported me has helped, but he isn't the brains behind everything I do, I am! The lack of support and love we give ourselves has a lifelong impact on not just ourselves but our kids too, because they see you putting yourself last, all back of the bus and shit, and they learn how to behave based on what they have seen. Do we want our kids to believe that little of themselves? Fuck no! So why do we allow it to happen in our own bodies? The places where life has grown, or passion has flared, and love blossomed. Why did we stop loving ourselves? Did we ever try? Probably not hard enough, and that's why it's important to be mindful of how we speak to ourselves and how we choose to love, including who we choose to love.

It'll never be our responsibility to make excuses for the bad guys and their shitty behaviour. I don't know where you start with loving yourself because the one thing I've learned about it is you can't teach something that is so different for every person. I felt like a cock for hugging myself every morning before I got out of bed and a lot of the time I didn't feel like it made a difference, saying how much I loved myself, and yet it was part of the process of finding the real me. She was under there somewhere, buried beneath all the horrible things I used to say about myself and all the time spent wishing that I was just normal.

What is normal? PAH! When you find out, can you give me a ring and let me know?? This idea of normal should have expired right along with eighties shoulder pads. There is no normal, and I think even more so in how we should view mental health. It is so vast and varied that I think it's almost impossible to know what would be considered as 'NORMAL'. Is it normal to think about something so horrific and devastating that you are reduced to tears and you wonder why and how the fuck your brain is so fucked up??!? Maybe not, and yet intrusive thoughts are very much a real thing, one that is so common they even made a fucking name for it. Intrusive thoughts! So, normal is almost impossible to gauge because we can't begin to figure out what someone went through to get to whatever point they find themselves in where they begin to be labelled abnormal, a freak, or a weirdo. I think if our internal thoughts were external, we'd soon realise how so many people are thinking similar things.

Why me? Why? It feels so unfair! I am a good person, I deserve to love myself. I hate this hurt. If only I could be that person! I wish I was more like . . . (enter name) . . . Does it sound familiar? We all think it, or at least I'm led to believe anyone in the pits of despair, or even mildly feeling like utter shit, feels like this and questions why. The truth behind it is, ultimately, despair does feel like a huge injustice and it does feel incredibly lonely, and it makes us look to other people, thinking, *Wow, they must be happier than me,* because they say they are, or because they smile and wear nice clothes. It's the devastating effect of being silent in our struggle, or not finding the right kind of people who can hear and understand where you're at. This isn't an overnight kind of thing; it's lifelong and we really do need to remember that. If it's not right to be forever dancing between 'I have fucking got this' and 'Fuck my life, what went wrong', then I really don't know what right actually is.

Expecting life to be a walk in the park, or striving for more money because it'll solve all your problems and make you happy, or finding the right guy who will make you feel good about yourself, is only shunting the problem along to the next goal post. The overall turd in the room is that no one has life nailed all the time. Yes, they might smile, but you know what, I can smile even on my shittest of days. It doesn't mean a fucking thing. Perfection won't ever be accomplished because there is nothing perfect about being a human. If there was I am sure as fuck we wouldn't have managed to end up with a prime minister like Boris fucking Johnson!

Giving away your power and energy for the benefit of other people will only ever help one person out – the other fucking person. If that one person is worth even one fucking ounce of your time and love, they will happily give that power back to you. They will want you to replenish your sad soul with all of the time it needs for it to feel whole again. Any fucker that challenges your needs has to be given the flick.

Anyone who isn't going to be your ride or die, any fucker who is going to talk behind your back, needs to be sent on their jolly fucking way, and any mood hoover that sucks you drier than my Dyson around Steve's knob needs to do one. You don't owe them a thing, you don't even owe them an explanation if you don't want to give it. Why should you? Again, where does the power lie if you are giving them the reason you barely feel strong enough to give? We don't belong to anyone through loyalty, or because of length of service. You aren't a washing machine that is still within its warranty, so why should you continue the very same, boring predictable loop of shamefully stepping on eggshells to keep up the appearance of happiness or even friendship? I think I could have always told you this, and no doubt somewhere nestled inside my other book these words are there, but they feel even more relevant this time around.

I have always used the phrases 'smashing into a million pieces' and then having to 'glue myself back together' differently, and I think when you have a mental health crisis or a breakdown, it is a form of a breakthrough because you do learn in time how resilient you actually are and that reminds you of how strong you are. It doesn't matter how messy it all looked and felt in the process of the shit mess you found yourself in, you just come out a redefined person because you are so aware that for every time these things happen, you have to be stronger. The amount of power and strength it takes to fall that hard and then survive it is indescribable. I know so many of you will be reading this and feeling every inch how hard it is to survive something no one else can see: your own demons.

I realise now that is exactly what mine were: demons that hung around in my mind like cobwebs that just needed to be swept away. I can't remove it, the trauma, the history. It's not something that just disappears. 'I fucking wish,' I hear you all cry. I think it's about the process of understanding the fact it's not yours. Those demons that you carry, or I carry, belong to someone else, and that is okay. You don't need to pretend to be brave and carry the weight of the world on your shoulders. Letting go sounds easy, but it's not. It is a process; it takes time and it'll always take kindness, which if you are anything like me comes in short supply when you are expected to give it to yourself.

The emotional wounds are unavoidable and there are days where I wake up wanting to cry because it will never feel fair. Fairness feels like a big part of this struggle. *Why? This shouldn't be happening to me!* So, who should it be happening to? *Anyone but me!* On those days I wouldn't care if someone else carried that pain because it feels crushingly unfair to be the one having to. I have had to face up to a lot this year; I think a lot of us have. Covid has been a pretty big wall to hit against, and I've seen so many people who have believed the wine in the garden with friends, the trip away with the family or the reunion of loved ones would change everything, and when it didn't they wondered what broke in those long days of lockdown. I think the pandemic made pretty much all of us sit with a whole lot of whatever we'd run away from, and to begin with it felt manageable, but as time went on it bit up in the arse a little harder until all of a sudden we couldn't just avoid it and we all had to acknowledge it.

The words 'acknowledge it' imply the tip of a hat at the train conductor as you step off the train going on to an adventure. HAHAHAAA, wouldn't it be nice for that shit to be THAT easy!! Where you just gave it the little nod and wink of the eye to say, 'Hey, I see you, and I'm on my merry way.' Acknowledging your problems requires a lot more strength than that, and it's something I have been dragged through kicking and fucking screaming because admitting what is glaringly obvious feels so much more painful than you think it would be.

I have learned to hold back my emotions at times when I should be showing them because to some people, my feelings would be inappropriate. I could quite easily cry after sex, for example. Why? Because my body struggles to work out the emotions for happy and sad. I can break down from laughing too hard at something. I get that many people experience this, but, fuck me, it often makes you feel like an outcast for not playing by the rules of what we often see on the TV. The beautiful endings where everyone lives happily ever after and nothing seems to hurt. We all want to gloss over the embarrassing parts where life doesn't feel quite so wonderful.

It's the slow and silent enemy and it ticks and ticks away under the skin. Do you often feel like you're completely alone? Like no one could possibly feel this awful? *No one would be friends with me if they really knew what I thought about myself.* I have and it's really hard to move past this idea that you are alone, because while it does in fact feel like a gaping hole of black, the worst part about it all is you do have to do all the work. Yes, people can help. They can look after the kids. They can cook the dinner, hug you and love you, but it all comes back to the fact that you do have to put all that hard work in, and it hurts because you didn't deserve for this to happen to you. You really didn't, my darling, and I'm so sorry you are being faced with how utterly shit it feels to be dragging yourself through it. I have been and am in it too, and I am still working on myself.

This isn't because I want you to feel doomed but more to realise this isn't some book from an inspiration wanker telling you that your life is just going to get better because you found your inner being. I want to be real about how hard it actually is. I feel like ignorance has played a huge part in how I would previously talk about my journey with mental health. I felt like I just didn't have to do the work any more, and now I realise I don't get that luxury. I will have to show up and do the work every single fucking day for the rest of my life. Why? Because I deserve my life. So do you! You deserve that happiness and self-belief, not that it'll be all sunshine and rainbows – that is completely unrealistic – but more that this self-acceptance isn't a million miles away, even if you believe you don't have the resources, or the time, or the energy. You do have all of those things; they might look different to mine or the next person's but you do need to invest that time into looking into why, what and how. You need to accept this isn't just going away and that you deserve to treat yourself better. As I have said so many times over, it is managing those triggers, working on your boundaries, pushing for the right kind of care (even if it is within the NHS) and understanding the fact that if you can't read, you can listen, and if you haven't got time, then you can follow accounts on social media that give you reasons to feel hope or clarity.

My level of self-worth in believing what I was entitled to has always been appallingly low and so being given the simple task of speaking nicely to myself seemed like an utterly fucking stupid idea because how can that be any good? How can that hold power? And yet it does, of course it does, and that is a resource you have there waiting to be used immediately. It does, however, take a lot of work, but is it worth it? You bet your fucking ass it is.

Does it actually end? I believe it's not so much an ending but more of an acceptance. You are here, and I will manage you like a wild mountain goat that just got leashed and is gagging to run away. I believe you can heal; actually I know you can. It isn't quick, it's slow and, put in the right hands of professionals or even self-investment, is one of the biggest jewels you can ever be given. The wild goat will always be there, but you'll know how to talk to it, calm it and understand it. You can't just one day say, 'Fuck it – I'm not going to suffer any more,' because if it was that simple I'm pretty sure no fucker would ever suffer with it. I have personally found the journey back-breaking at times and so slow that, somewhere, even a snail is looking over its shoulder sniggering.

I am a mum. It's a pretty important job to me, one which I generally take seriously although I often lack many fucks to really put too much effort in. The title of 'mum' comes with many responsibilities, but coming at the bottom of the pile should not be one of them.

Piles are not only found in my washing basket but my arse too, and they both lead to a lot of pain and anguish over which gets treated first, but the bottom line is . . . I do. Why? Because it isn't selfish, but it is necessary and essential to be a better person to your kids. We can all give a google of the things that make the most effective parent, or how to bake the perfect birthday cake, but the answers of who you need to be aren't in Google; they're in you.

I should, however, say Google is a dodgy place. It can be helpful and completely fucking vile in only making you feel a million times worse. I gave this wonderful advice in my last book about how I googled positive stories of the antidepressants I was on and how they made me realise I wasn't alone and how much it helped. Well, here is a little update. That didn't happen the second time, and what I saw instead was a lot of horror stories of people 12 weeks into their medication still feeling like utter shit. Well, when you're on day three and the end of your arsehole has fallen out onto the floor because your life feels so dire, reading SOMEONE ELSE'S experience of what they went through is not helpful. Mainly because (can you see the clue?) it is someone else's experience. That is like expecting to go to a restaurant and everyone liking the same dish. That is never going to fucking happen and that goes for the reality of getting help. One thing that helps one person isn't going to be the next person's fixer. You can't expect one person to be your awakening and enlightenment because they took the same medication you did.

So, I say all this, totally going back on the shit that worked for me last time (which to be fair could work for you, but call this your balance). Sometimes it does jack shit and you have to find something to help you feel stronger. And making sure you know what you are looking at, reading and learning isn't damaging you further is a very important life lesson. One thing I found fascinating about some of the forums (this is speaking in hindsight because I found nothing fascinating at the time; I just felt shit) was that there were people years on from having started taking their antidepressants still there, encouraging and helping complete strangers to not give up hope. I mean, it was actually quite incredible and something I would have previously done to make sure no one felt alone in what they were going through, but actually being that person to someone else is majorly draining and exhausting.

We all have a mental load to prop up, but if there is one thing I have learned about myself it's that all that ever did was make me escape my own problems. Sometimes other people's shit feels more important than our own.

We aren't alone even though there are some days when it completely feels like it. You'll go to bed and think, *Tomorrow will be a better day,* and then you wake up and think, *Oh fuck off!! Why am I not over this already?!* Just be kind to yourself and know the bad moments will always pass. (Says she who, when in the bad moments, screams and cries, 'This is it, I definitely won't feel better this time!!' I believe I am completely the person to say this, though, because I have been there enough times to say it will and does pass. It isn't forever but those days are so long, and the road through them feels like a massive cup of hot shit on your face.)

On a daily basis, I see women messaging me, yearning for the solution that will ultimately fix them, and I hear how desperate they are; I feel it too. I can understand that level of despair; it hurts deeper than anything ever will, and sometimes that hurt needs to be there to be heard, and listened to. I think the labels of mental health issues are kind of handed out like sweets on Halloween. It's like we get to say, 'Oh, I have mental health issues,' and that's it. No backstory; it almost serves as an excuse as to why we don't show up to events, or cancel last-minute, or lose friends, or struggle to hold down relationships, but it never really reaches the core of why?? What happened? How did you arrive here? Something so awful must have happened to you for you to be here, looking for the reasons why you can't manage the life you want and why your mental health holds you back.

I don't want my history to serve as my future, do you? I want my life to be fuller, happier, and I want to know and believe I deserve it. Don't you want that too? So, believe. Believe in you, and nothing else. It is okay, and lean into the fear of the things that feel too much to achieve, no matter how small they feel to others. Your steps, your journey, will never, ever look like anyone else's and that is why there is no quick fix in life. There is no easy solution to overcoming being in your head too much. You have to find your groove, and be at peace with the fact that, as you look after your own well-being, you will be better able to care for others and more easily build the life you want for yourself.

How do you begin to wrap up something that still feels so open and raw? How do I begin to send you on your merry way into life feeling like a new person with new hopes when I have heavily ladened this book with the really harsh realities of mental health? I think the thing is, life is always going to be hard, and sometimes it's good to understand the fact there is no straightforward approach to surviving it. I have read books that have boasted that they will give you the ability to change your life if you commit to it, and yet reading those books has given me more anxiety because all it has felt like in that moment is a long, endless list of impossible tasks where you reach for the stars and don't look down.

You can't begin to reach for the stars if you don't believe your feet can leave the ground. The point of any form of recovery is you do have to start from the ground up. The harder you work at each stage of this, the higher you will fly. I am not implying you'll become the next Elon Musk, but I am saying you are capable of much bigger things, with more positive focus, if you just begin to believe in who you are. The fact you are still hanging around the friends you had 20 years ago with little to no connection but loyalty keeping you there only pushes the idea that you are limited to the people you believe you are meant to be around, rather than knowing there are other friendships out there that will ignite your soul and feed your mind. You don't need to stay in relationships with men because you feel they're the only people who will love you. You have the power to love yourself more than anyone else ever could. You can healthily implement the boundaries you've been desperate to have with family because you need space, for you! You are allowed that, and that isn't you being selfish; it's actually really nourishing. Boundaries won't always be liked by others, but that's okay. Friends won't always stick around, and that shows growth. Change is healthy, self-love is valuable, getting help shows strength.

You are wonderful, you are loving, worthy and courageous. If reading this book has spoken to a part of you that you realise needs to be heard then I'm pleased. I wanted this to be honest, I needed this to be raw. I am very much learning on the job about how to manage life and accept that all that shit I carry can sometimes feel heavy, and you know what? It's alright for that to be the case. It is completely okay to just acknowledge your path has been rougher than my hairy husband's arse.

I hope you take the opportunity to love yourself a little more gently and take a little more time to figure out what you want! What do you need? How can you help yourself? I think you are amazing; for a start you've picked up this book and decided to invest in a little story about my life and how I would love and hope to help you change how you see yourself. I hope it has ignited a fire in your belly due to how much we as women face injustice on a daily basis and why that feels so unfair. I hope it has given you the opportunity to re-evaluate friendships, relationships and family. I hope it has given you the chance to see you are much stronger than you realise and deserve so much more kindness than you allow yourself. I want you to love you; I want you to want you and love you because you're allowed to, because you're entitled to.

One last thing . . .

What I would like this next page to be is the one you tear out of the book. Fucking do it!! Now!! Alright, maybe read it first, but what I'd like you to do with it is keep it, pass it on but most of all make sure it is used for what it was intended and that is to fill someone with hope! Granted, I feel for the person in the charity shop that is reading this book and hasn't got this page, but they're shit out of luck.

I will get through this . . .

I am fucking awesome.

You go, girl, you bad-ass bitch.

I think you are the mutt's bollocks.

I love myself.

I forgive myself.

I am learning.

I am a work in progress.

My life is going to get better.

I deserve to heal.

I deserve to be around people who feed my soul.

What other affirmations would you choose for yourself?

_____

_____

_____

_____

_____

_____

NO SHAME

Hang it, stick it, hold it, keep it, pass it on but most of all keep repeating it to yourself. Change the words to fit your thang, and don't give up on it. You don't have to love everything about yourself tomorrow, but you do need to start working on it today.

Just remember, when all feels lost, you fucking got this.

Xx

P.S. I love you, and thank you for being here.

CHAPTER 10

It'll All Be Alright in the End

FUCCCKKKK, I can't believe I've done it. What does it all sum up to be in the end? The fact you can't win it all, you will have to learn to make room for improvement and while change for some doesn't feel like anything they need, for others it is a necessity to survival. The shackles around our ankles of fear, rejection and shame have meant we stopped living and carried on existing. It feels exhausting, it feels tiring, but you aren't a million miles away from making the load that little bit lighter.

This is all fighting talk and I might end on a high by saying, 'WWWWAAAAHHHHHH, life is solved!' Well, it's not and it'll never be that easy but it most definitely doesn't have to be that fucking hard either. You have exceptional taste in books, this I know for a given, but more to the point you will have read this one for a good reason. Was it because you follow me on social media? Or that you randomly found me in among a shelf of other books? Either way, the whole point of anything I ever write is the hope it'll help and educate someone. Bravery and openness come from being present among people (mainly women) who can appreciate everything you are saying and why you are saying it.

Ending this book, I can see the journey it has been on with me, and I hope you have been able to go through it with me too. I started this book with a sense of lost direction. I wondered, *How can I make this book the one I always wanted to write?* While also being so terrified of what people might think, and while feeling that heavy shame of what people would read about me, and then potentially judge me for?

I have been on an experience of self-discovery while writing this, I have sat in my dining room day after day, working through this process while still recovering from my breakdown. I would like to see this book as the breakthrough of my breakdown. It is an account of how brave anyone can be if they just hold on to the things that feel important and learn to gently let go of the things that don't belong to them.

We don't realise how much we cling to through fear and shame. We have learned to live the lives of everyone else around us, through their stories or even their own fears and doubts. Shame shapes us into the people we are, but it also has the power to break us into the people we didn't want to be. It is just okay to acknowledge and remember we are people who deserve love and praise.

I have spoken bravely about my journey, my story, and I hope it will give you the courage to do the same. You will always be allowed to find new paths, new relationships and happier friendships. Our lives aren't set in concrete, they are forever changing and we aren't ever going to manage to get through life without there being some casualties. We will fall in and out of love, we will find new friends and we will move on from situations that served us no good. It's okay to learn to let go of those things, but you can't do that or feel worthy of that if you don't start to believe you are allowed it.

No matter who that person is – your sister, best mate, cousin, husband – sometimes it's okay to just acknowledge that a relationship needs time and space to give you the opportunity to grow. You are allowed to flourish and thrive.

I have never felt the passion of sharing the truth more than I do now. I am so proud of myself for how far I have come in such a short space of time in relation to the rest of my life, even though when I was in it, I felt like every hour took a lifetime to pass by. It's a place I hope I never find myself in again. No matter how hard life might feel at the time, I have promised myself that I deserve more than I ever gave myself before.

We really do deserve to see ourselves in more light than we allow. As women, we are pigeonholed constantly and I am SO tired of how little we fight back against those ideas. The fact men are glamorised constantly for looking after their children, rewarded with praise, a promise of a beer and a blow job, all the while women do the same day in, day out, with no notice and no rewards. No one ever turns around to the mother and says, 'Thank you for looking after your children,' and yet it happens all the time with men. I hate this, because it only further confirms the idea that a women's main job is to parent, while in this day and age she should also find the time to hold down a job. We take the day's leave when the kids are sick; we are always flexible over holidays, and we still fight for any form of equal pay. This is continuing to recycle the same idea and that is that women aren't as strong or able as men. When in actual fact this world would be fucked without us. It would be fucked without men too, but no one is questioning that fact, and yet the simple act of underpaying women and completely overlooking their rights and safety is making us all believe we have to fight harder for the things men automatically get in life.

This world expects so much of women. In the most underhanded way possible, it is expecting small girls to fit into certain sizes for their age, with next to no real flex given to how girls' bodies change differently as they grow. The subliminal message we send to girls for needing the next size up at age four is 'you are too big', not that the clothing industry is completely fucked. It demands the same pretty pink perfection that was expected of the 1940s housewife. We don't have to change the world; we just need to learn to change our own approach to protect ourselves but also think more of ourselves to know we do deserve more.

I have spent a lifetime running away from everything I didn't like about myself and I don't know how much energy I wasted doing something that literally got me nowhere. I can't avoid the reality of my life.

I can't escape the fact I was forced to grow up far quicker than I ever should have done. I am a survivor of things I wouldn't wish on anyone, but I survived it because I am strong. Even when I felt like I was weak, I was actually exceptionally strong and I lacked so much kindness towards myself. I have learned and taught myself things that have the ripple effect that goes on into my children because I am able to teach them the things I have picked up along the way. I want to give them the chance at a life where they understand how to return to their own body and love it no matter how it arrives in life. I want them to know they are in control of who they are, no one else.

I think these things I am able to pass on to my children right now are the gifts I probably always needed to give them. Along with all the love I have always provided, this is what matters the most to me. After my panicked call to 999 threatening to take my life, I have lived in this fear, waiting for social services to call, because losing my children is all I ever imagined. I would get a random phone call and I would pick it up, expecting it to be someone from child and family services. They never called, they never checked in on the kids, or me. I felt relieved at the time, but now looking back I wish they had. While that would have been a hurt I carried for the rest of my life, it would have been a potential for them to be given the extra support we might have not been able to give them. We all hear 'social services' and automatically think that means we'll lose our children, but in actual fact it's more about making sure the children's care is the priority.

I look back now and feel like the person all that happened to was someone else, and she was. I will never be her again; I know too much now. I have been able to link all the traumatic events in my life to why I have behaved the way I have. I don't need anyone to analyse that for me, or question me for it. I am just allowed to own it. I am allowed to just say these things happened. I was sexually abused, I have allowed toxic relationships to go on longer than I should have, and none of that was okay. I am okay with the fact I don't have to live with those demons any more. I don't have to carry the burden of things that aren't mine to own. I don't have to explain my reasons if I don't want to, I get to just call time and space on the things that feel too much.

There is a level of freedom, even as I write all of this. It's almost like I have more room in my lungs to breathe; things feel less heavy. Life isn't always going to feel like this and I know my mental health is a juggle I will need to always make a priority. I will without a doubt have times in my life where I forget the fact I should and need to come first. I will forget the fact I have to focus on my own body and mind, and it'll take me a hot minute to come back to the things in my life that I am lacking. But I know one thing and that is I never, ever want to go back to that dark place again. I don't want to hunt for the torch in the darkness, and I shouldn't have to. I have been punished enough for the actions of other people and I don't deserve to allow that for myself again.

I spent a long time believing I should be punished. I can't tell you why, or what for. I just believed deep down I was a terrible person and that I just wasn't strong enough to be like the people I looked up to. I don't want to look up to anyone any more, no celebrities, no friends or family. I just want to see myself as equal with all the chance at happiness they have. Sure, our lives look different. I am not J.Lo, but I've realised how empty it is to wish for a life like that. Why would I believe I would be happy just because I was someone else? I wouldn't, and that self-comparison is always going to be there, but I just need to remember I am not that person and that is a good thing because I am me instead and that me is more than enough. I am changing, evolving, learning new things and changing the way I tackle life. I want to give myself all the things I have given away to everyone else and that is my own version of happiness. It is dysfunctional, it might not always make sense to anyone else, but it makes sense to me, which will always be the most important thing.

We never really acknowledge ourselves because we are more often than not looking at how we can improve or how we wished we were someone else. I have been that person for such a long time and I realise I have done something some people don't ever do in their whole lifetime and that is finding myself.

When will it be your time to find yourself? When the kids are in school? Why? I think it's your time now! We don't have to put ourselves on the back-burner all the time. We don't have to miss out on life because someone else takes the priority. You are important too, you are allowed to dream, you are allowed to do the things that make you happy, even if that's buying a vibrator. Do it! Make the small changes, learn to love who you are. Do you more often than not find reasons to start something in a week, a month? Next Monday? More than likely, and I'm not talking about the fucking diet either. I'm talking about the promise of something for yourself. You are just allowed to work towards making that something you do now.

I see now why the diet industry is so set up to fail women and that is because it feeds the insecurities of women who believe they need to change. How can you possibly begin to change the outside of your presence when the inside of you is so riddled with the worries that you aren't good enough? How can you reach a goal weight when all you believe is that you'll fail anyway? Where is the diet that positively works on your self-esteem while it works on how you see yourself? Diets aren't designed that way because if they were, they would fix the issue, and that is your own personal self-belief. If they fixed that, they wouldn't make money from telling you that you needed to lose more weight, or that you needed to push a little harder.

I know so many of you will be drawn in by the diet fads and I want to tell you before you close this book to not buy into the bullshit. If you want to change the outside, work on the inside first. I think that's the saddest part about our society – that we weren't raised to see ourselves as worthy; we were raised to believe we always had to prove something to someone, none more so than ourselves, and then once we had proven that point we felt this need to prove some more and so, as life ticks by, we spend the time we have constantly trying to convince everyone we are strong enough, kind enough, brave enough, good enough, sexy enough, loving enough. Well, enough is enough! The time on our limited self-existence is up and it's the era of telling ourselves something a little kinder, to make us a little stronger, to teach us how to love ourselves a little longer.

283

You deserve this, we all do. We deserve the life we believe we can't get because we think we're too old or too stuck in the middle. I hope above all else you come away from this book knowing that I have been where you are, and I have believed about myself what you believe but I have made it through. I know how I got here, I worked hard for it. I do deserve it and I will continue to fight for the fact I owe myself this piece of the life I worked for. It isn't just for Steve or our kids to enjoy. It's mine.

Take little moments for yourself and put your self-care first. They don't need to be grand, they don't need to be aspirational to anyone else, they just need to be a tiny goal for you to want to achieve for yourself:

Get up earlier – even if it's five minutes, force yourself up. It will be hard. I get it, I am the owl and I don't do mornings, but I notice the difference in myself when I lie in bed too long.

Make your bed – I get it but, fuck me, that little bit of order of a duvet that's been quickly put back where it belongs does make you feel good when you walk back into the room and see it.

Drink – not vodka. Water, and stay hydrated. Your body sometimes thinks it doesn't need these things when it's at its worst but in actual fact not doing these things is bypassing the most important part of self-care.

Write it down – whatever it is, just write it out, and while I have said this already, I will say it again. Make a book of the good stuff, make a book of the bad stuff. You need a space that is made up purely of the good things that make you feel safe or loved, then make sure you keep the good and bad separate. Once the bad book is full, throw it, rip it up, fucking burn it but don't keep it. Learn to let that bad stuff go.

Eat something that makes you feel good and work on why you don't need to feel bad for it. I get that could be a challenge but work on it.

Go outside and get out of your head.

Breathe – you're already an expert at it so just notice how good you are at it.

Move – even when you don't want to, because it'll be the thing that in months to come you'll be thankful you forced yourself to do.

And breathe some more!

I have come a long way, even from the start of this book. My anxiety was so high, and I was deliberately avoiding telling my psychologist about writing this because I was so scared she would say this was a bad idea. Instead when I eventually plucked up the courage to say, 'Look, I'm kind of writing a fucking book behind your back and I feel like a massive dick because I don't think I am good enough to tell this story,' she just said, 'And is this something you want to do?' I realised I had been waiting on someone to tell me no. I was wanting the permission of someone who seemed more grown-up than me to just say, 'Yeah, do it.' I needed that reassurance and as soon as she asked the question of 'Is it what you want to do?' I knew in that moment, yes, this is what I wanted to do. She asked me why. And I said, 'Because this is my story; this has been something I have had to live with for all of my life and I have carried the shame of it like shackles and it has dictated so much of my life without me even realising it.'

I have spent all my energy and strength trying to protect others from something I had no control over. I was trying to make sure no one ever hurt like I did, while seeing them hurt because that's life sometimes and then feeling this weird sense of failure for not saving them or doing things differently. I have wasted so many years on the permission and approval of everyone else, and I had no idea how to just give that to myself.

I had grown to become a mum who couldn't trust people to look after my children for fear of them hurting or abusing them, when I couldn't keep them safe. I have been swamped with some of the most disturbingly intrusive thoughts that I felt like I needed to be locked up and would cry myself to sleep at night thinking I was such a freak and no one could ever understand. I carried these secrets and they burdened me with some of the heaviest baggage, which I just learned to carry more of, like my punishment for being abused was to keep on hurting and to continue being punished for something so cruel and evil that I've never been able to escape it.

Even as I finish this book, I am faced with the fact I need to tell friends and family what it's about. I haven't found that courage yet, but I think that probably speaks volumes as to what it feels like to live the life of someone who has been violated; you struggle to find the voice you need to speak up. It is really easy to say to anyone, 'But why didn't you say something? Why didn't you speak up sooner?' The reality is the manipulation that goes on during any time of abuse is the reason why these things happen too often and last longer than they ever should.

As a child, I ended up believing, because of the things I was told by my abuser, that I had no choice but to put up with my abuse and be quiet, and I have taken that subconscious manipulation into adulthood and never known how to let it go, almost like that was part of my DNA. How can you know there is another version of yourself that is whole and inwardly loved when you never had the pleasure of meeting her?

Well, I can now say I have met her. She is wonderful. She is still struggling, she doesn't always like herself and she makes a lot of mistakes with regards to her self-care, but she is taking a bit more time to find herself. She likes things without someone else needing to tell her it's okay to like them. She is finding her feet as this person who is allowed to do whatever she wants.

The quiet, moody teen in me that never got to rebel is doing everything she ever wanted now; she finally understands why she was so scared of boys as a girl and struggled to want to let go and be sexually wild, and she is learning to accept why that's okay. Because she just wanted to keep herself safe, she wanted to avoid any further damage at the hands of a man. This teen girl inside me that wants to sleep around and be wild and free is doing as she pleases (without the sleeping around part). She is cutting all her hair off and giving herself an undercut. She is covering herself with tattoos and piercings, and she is saying 'fuck it' at every given opportunity. She is less anxious, which has meant she has eaten more food, and has gained more weight than she ever has done before, and she is trying to make sense of that.

She is going to be okay, and she is going to get through this. She is making sure every step she takes is towards a life that means she never, ever has to face other people's demons that somehow managed to sneak into her body and hang around her mind.

I have always kind of yo-yoed with my weight, but I've never been more than a size 14. I can lose weight really quickly but that has usually been a direct result of my anxiety. I didn't realise until recently that two years ago I had an almost constant tight feeling of pain across my chest. From the moment I woke to the moment I went to sleep. To even acknowledge the pain or the anxiety only made that feeling stronger. I realise now that I actually very rarely have that feeling these days. I have been freed of the pain anxiety caused me daily, and while that doesn't mean I have found the cure to never feeling it again, it's more that I now see how important it is to only ever make that pain a visitor and not a lodger in my body. I don't deserve it. I deserve more and owe myself more. I want to give myself all the chances in life to just feel loved and be loved without the question . . . 'but do I really deserve it?' Trusting the people I know will be there, no matter what, without question – in my moments of doom but also in my moments of triumph, who aren't too busy to clap me on my way up or even to hug me on my way down. I want and need that love in my life and I really can't stress enough how it's become a huge priority for me to maintain that level of trust and love.

I wanted to write this book because I can. I wish I had written it years ago; I wish I could have let go of all the things that held me back and felt too much to cope with. I do live with regret because I feel part of my life has been wasted trying to really be something I wasn't. I tried to not be broken even though I was. I have kissed goodbye to the moments in motherhood that I should have been entitled to, the cuddles and skin-to-skin where I didn't feel this need to reject it or try to remove myself from it. I still find it hard to move past that, because it fucking hurts. I didn't carry two kids for nine months at a time, then push them out of my unreasonably small hole, to never want to hold or kiss them. I love them so much and I would do anything to keep them safe; I want those moments back and I am having to speak to myself more kindly when those feelings come up, because I can't change them and, yes, they were robbed from me, which was completely unfair but it doesn't change the fact I still turned out to be an amazing mum to my boys. I still managed to give them my all; even when I had nothing to give,

I still found something just for them. Nothing will ever define the love of a parent quite like that, and seeing them love me even when I wasn't able to get out of bed, how they cared for and nurtured me, has shown me what an amazing mum they have. What a powerful statement to make about yourself, and yet it's true.

They used to be my reason for carrying on. So did Steve. I pinned so many of my life expectations on them and their happiness that there must have been some kind of pressure felt within their lives to live up to what I had hoped for them. I have recognised that in myself and realised that what they need me to be is just me! They need me to thrive for who I am; they want me to be my reason for carrying on. Loving and living for who you are doesn't make you selfish; it makes you worthy of the power you hold within yourself.

You don't need anyone else; they are the things that make you smile and make you happy, but the things already inside you are what make you whole and the rest is the bonus. No, we aren't taught this so it's something we have to learn for ourselves, and no one will make room for it in our lives but us. You make the time to save yourself from the life that might feel heavy, or the things that might feel too much; you have to prioritise the things that you need to make space for in your own life.

Stop being afraid of the things people might think or say about you for making yourself the reason why you smile. Those people – and it really doesn't matter who they are – can get fucked. They can take a step back out of their own arsehole and they will need to get over it. Why? Because you count, you matter and sometimes it's about doing all the things you thought you'd never do that will make you find the you that's always been there, waiting to be found.

So, I end this book with a wish and that is that the person who started this book so unsure, completely washed away by the trauma of surviving all the shit she has learned to live with, continues to grow. I want to keep changing, evolving and learning. I want to talk more openly about the things that really do feel too taboo to open up about. I want to just let the good things in, and breathe out the bad stuff.

The future feels uncertain, not helped by the pandemic, but I think I am still swimming in the territory of surviving and not quite trusting myself to stay afloat because I don't want to be so cocky that I go back under. For now, I want to enjoy this moment in time where I can just say to myself, 'I fucking did it.' You can too: I have worked to get my life back, and my career on track. I've not stopped wanting to write this book; even when I thought I had run out of words, I kept writing because I want to succeed. I don't mean that in the really fucking toxic, high-pressure sense of performing and achieving; I mean I want to reach for all the things I ever wanted and I just want to know I'm allowed them. No one will be there waiting to rob me of them, because I deserve them; I deserve this. *This* moment – where I type the final sentences in a book I wrote about the things I have kept quiet all my life. I have been the brave one who wanted to share something that is really hard, that has an endless amount of shame surrounding it, and I am prepared for the fact I might get asked questions that make me feel uncomfortable, but I have built myself up to a place where I am strong enough to say, 'I don't want to talk about that.' I am allowed and entitled to just be me, and to surround myself with only the people who love who I am.

Everything I have written is for you, the person who survived the things that were designed to destroy her, but they didn't. You kept on, you didn't give up and you survived. No matter how that looks right now, no matter what you might feel and how broken you may think you are as a direct result of the things you have lived with, just know you are still here because you were strong.

We won't completely get through life unscathed and we all deal with trauma differently, but we have entered into an era where your voice is allowed to be heard, the stories you tell aren't unworthy and your survival and struggle should be celebrated and not demonised. The most important thing to always remember is that whether or not you choose to share your story is your choice! There is no right or wrong answer to it.

One of the heavy things I have had to consider in writing this book is my boys. The fact they will learn of what happened to me at some point in their lives when they're older because the words in this book exist. It has been a real tussle for me, because I worry about how that could impact them. The shame and embarrassment of knowing that about your mum and wishing you didn't know it. Where is the line, though? Where I get to live and let go of the things that weren't my fault and move on? The reason I pushed on with this book is the fact I shouldn't have to hide it like a dirty secret. I shouldn't be ashamed of what happened, and so I hope when my boys are in fact older, they can understand why this was so important for me! To be not only a mum, but more importantly the mum who decided she wanted to be defined by more than just the job title of being a mother. I wonder how many other mums keep the secret? For fear of it causing damage to their children, all the while it damages us for carrying it. I really have seen how I have changed the way I parent now that I have a better understanding, a little more personal perspective and respect for the fact that not only am I me before I am their mum, but they also are their own people. The challenge of raising human beings is huge and at times it feels suffocating, but this experience, this situation, this story, felt massively important to me. I wanted and needed to make sure it all got told.

Wherever you are, whatever life you are living, just try to make sure you live it for you, with the deep understanding that this doesn't make you selfish. You are a work in progress, give yourself a pat on the back. You're getting there, babes.

You don't owe anyone anything, you don't need to be the person everyone expects you to be. You just need to gently learn all the wonderful things about yourself that got you here.

I will end with one last list for you to make – your 'fuck it' list.

The moments where you go 'Fuck it! I am making it happen!' 'Fuck it, I'm eating it!' 'Fuck it, I am going on the date!' 'Fuck it, I am masturbating tonight.'

The big fat 'fuck it' of beyond.

I love my 'fuck it' moments; they make up all the many moments in recent times where I have done something I would have never done before, taken risks and realised I get to be me just once and I want to get to live out my days the way I want to and not in the way other people expect.

I guess it could be your bucket list, but 'fuck it' list sounds cooler and less doom and gloom.

Let it be known that, from this day forward, you . . . (enter name) . . . will learn to give fewer fucks about what others think and try to remember why she is fucking wonderful.

This has no expiration date to it either, so be sure to remind yourself regularly, as well as others around you who also might forget the fact they don't own you and your thoughts.

I am so proud of you.

A LITTLE UPDATE . . .

Before I end this book, I wanted to give you a little update, because the person who started writing this isn't the person finishing it. Yes, it's obviously still Laura, but I mean emotionally I have changed. I began with a real sense of anxiety over whether I was mentally well enough to even discuss the issues I have talked about here, and I feel immensely proud of the journey I have been on with this book. So, the update of where I am right now as I fill in the final pages . . .

I had mentioned at the beginning of this book that I was on sleeping medication. Well, it took me around five months, but I am now officially off the sleeping tablets and managing my sleep well. I do still struggle to get off to sleep, which can make me feel panicked, but I am actually managing to maintain that panic with a lot of self-soothing talk.

I am still very much in therapy, doing EMDR. I have been going at it on a mostly weekly basis for over a year now. It's been pretty intense but it's helping me, which is all I really care about. I want to keep those inner demons at bay for as long as possible, but as I've already mentioned, I know I will need therapy on and off for the rest of my life in order to keep myself sane. Well, as sane as I'll ever be.

I'm still medicated under the supervision of my doctor, and to be honest fuck knows what the future holds with that one. I don't even know what my wish might be going forward with regards to coming off it. I will keep plodding along and figuring that one out as I go and shrug off any shame surrounding medication.

I have had some real 'fuck it' moments ('fuck it' meaning I'm just taking the plunge and having a go at something I would have never dared to do before) since starting to write this book, and I feel like maybe writing has helped me to be brave enough to get lots of tattoos, do a sexy naked shoot and cut all my hair off. I have realised now more than ever that my life is so precious, and it is to be lived for me and me alone. All the right kinds of people in my life will support that in me and watch me flourish rather than try to suffocate my spirit.

I have chosen a much more brutally honest approach to my social media pages in a bid to keep a promise to myself, and that is if it's important enough to me, then it's important to share. That's because I have spent such a large proportion of my life being silent, people-pleasing and not really knowing how to be authentically me that I now have made a pledge to the inner child in me who deserves a happy and safe life that we/her/I will spend the rest of our lives looking after ourselves with more compassion and love than ever.

I am a completely different person because I had to be. My approach to maintaining my life used to be to take a pill and make it all go away, but I have learned it just doesn't work that way. I wonder how I could have been that ignorant for so long, but as with a lot of things, I have learned to forgive myself for not getting help sooner and to let go of the 'what might have been' from the past because I can't change it. These days, I am more about focusing on the here and now of what I am able to change.

Yoga, breath work, positive affirmations, trauma-based grounding techniques, colouring in, gardening and walking have all been such important tools to help me find my feet again, alongside therapy. I never, ever would have thought the things so simple in life could be a gateway to balancing my mental health. None of that has been easy. For a start, you have to believe in the process for it to even begin, and then you have to promise yourself a time and space where you dedicate yourself to looking after you. That is pretty fucking hard to do when you feel so unworthy that you believe it won't make a difference, or that you don't deserve it.

NO SHAME

I have been there, and I have had to learn the hard way. I really am just so proud of where I have come to in my life, and while the future scares the shit out of me, I am working on acknowledging that the future can wait because I want to learn to live in the here and now.

I don't want this to come across as an 'I'm fixed' ending because honestly, I don't believe there is enough fucking superglue in this world to ever really fix me, but I am accepting of the fact I will always work on it, and I'm kind of here for that. I am open to the fact I will always need to work at maintaining my own mental health – maybe more than others, but hey, I will continue to show up and be present enough to give it a good fucking go.

Acknowledgements

Firstly, I shall start by saying this book wouldn't exist without the talent, brains and dedication of everyone at Ebury. Sara and Lydia, you have nurtured me from the early days as an unconfident author trying to believe in her work, and I will be forever grateful for all your time and support. I would also like to give the biggest thanks to Sarah, my sub-editor, who was the person that gently reassured me to write exactly what I was holding back about. We have spent hours on the phone talking about so many different issues and ideas. She is one of the reasons why this book is so brutally honest and unashamedly candid. She believed in me and I felt every inch of that belief. I owe so much of my confidence as a writer to Ebury.

There is no denying the fact that without my therapist I probably wouldn't be here anymore, and while I kind of continue to fan that flame that I am obsessed with her still. I can't get through this acknowledgment without thanking Elena for everything she has done and continues to do for me in therapy. Yeah, that's right, I'm still in therapy. So, I did get to the end of this book and haven't managed to cut the umbilical cord from therapy yet. I am okay with that, though.

My family have continued to support me through the highs and lows of life. They have also had to live through every breakdown I have experienced and never been able to take away the pain or fear, but they haven't waivered in their support. This book hasn't been easy for anyone, because it is having to relive something we all had to endure to different degrees, and yet they have only championed me in telling my story.

Eva, I wouldn't be functioning in life without you. You simply saved my life and while I know you don't like that saying because you feel you didn't do enough, I am here to say you did and that you continue to be more of a friend than I could have ever wished for.

Lyndz and Vic, my oldest friends who have never stopped cheering me on, you have loved me even when I've not felt very lovable and you've been by my side since we were four.

Vic, you are my partner in crime, my wingman, my business partner, a friend I found through sheer luck and you've changed my life in so many ways. You've helped me to believe in myself more, you were one of the only people I called to talk to in the midst of my breakdown and you just get me on a level most people don't.

So many more friends to thank like Carly, Jools, Claire, Chara, Hannah and Helen, who have all for different reasons been so crucial in my recovery. Even if it's been the person to make sure doctors called me back, to sitting and listening to my rambles, or checking in to make sure I am okay. These people are the ones who have repeatedly caught me when I've fallen and I really haven't a fucking clue where I would be without them.

I am also so thankful for you, the person reading this book, because it means a lot and I'm not sure there will ever come a day when this opportunity to write about the things I feel so passionately about will ever get boring for me. So thank you for just being here. Your presence is more than enough and sometimes it's good to be told that.

I get to the last part and it is the biggest love and thanks to Steve, Elliott and Toby. My boys. The people who are my reason for fighting, for pushing on ahead and never giving up, even when things hurt. I will never own enough words to describe the wonder of these people in my life. They love me for who I am, they support me in whatever I do and even in my darkest moments they never left my side. To share a life with these humans is everything and more I could have ever asked for.

I chose to dedicate this book to every survivor, to every unspoken need and all the unheard pain that victims of abuse suffer. The strength to show up and continue to fight for yourself is unimaginable. No matter how bruised and battered life has made you feel, I want you to know I see you, I understand and I'm really proud of you. Let's never give up on ourselves.

x

Mental Health
Services Directory

MENTAL HEALTH

SAMARITANS

Telephone: 116 123 (24 hours a day, free to call)

Email: jo@samaritans.org

Website: https://www.samaritans.org

Provides confidential, non-judgemental emotional support for people experiencing feelings of distress or despair, including those that could lead to suicide. You can phone, email, write a letter or in most cases talk to someone face to face.

MIND INFOLINE

Telephone: 0300 123 3393 (9am–6pm Monday to Friday) or text 86463

Email: info@mind.org.uk

Website: www.mind.org.uk/information-support/ helplines

Mind provides confidential mental health information services.

With support and understanding, Mind enables people to make informed choices. The Infoline gives information on types of mental health problems, where to get help, drug treatments, alternative therapies and advocacy. Mind works in partnership with around 140 local Minds providing local mental health services.

RETHINK MENTAL ILLNESS ADVICE LINE
Telephone: 0808 801 0525 (1–4pm Monday to Friday; webchat service 9.30am–4pm Monday to Friday)
Email: advice@rethink.org
Website: http://www.rethink.org/about-us/our-mental-health-advice
Provides expert advice and information to people with mental health problems and those who care for them, as well as giving help to health professionals, employers and staff. Rethink also runs Rethink services and groups across England.

SANELINE
Telephone: 0300 304 7000 (4.30pm–10.30pm)
Website: www.sane.org.uk/what_we_do/support/helpline

Saneline is a national mental health helpline providing information and support to people with mental health problems and those who support them.

THE MIX

Telephone: 0808 808 4994 (4pm–11pm, free to call)
Email: Helpline email form
Crisis Support: Text 'THEMIX' to 85258
Website: www.themix.org.uk/get-support
The Mix provides judgement-free information and support to young people aged 13–25 on a range of issues including mental health problems. Young people can access the Mix's support via phone, email, webchat, peer-to-peer and counselling services.

SIDE BY SIDE

Website: https://sidebyside.mind.org.uk
Side by Side is an online community where you can listen, share and be heard. Side by Side is run by Mind.

SHOUT

Shout is the UK's first 24/7 text service, free on all major mobile networks, for anyone in crisis anytime, anywhere. It's a place to go if you're struggling to cope and you need immediate help.

Text: 85258
Website: https://www.giveusashout.org/

CHILDHOOD ABUSE

HELP FOR ADULT VICTIMS OF CHILD ABUSE (HAVOCA)
Website: https://www.havoca.org
Information and support for adults who have experienced any type of childhood abuse, run by survivors.

THE NATIONAL ASSOCIATION FOR PEOPLE ABUSED IN CHILDHOOD (NAPAC)
Telephone: 0808 801 0331
Email: support@napac.org.uk
Website: https://napac.org.uk
Supports adult survivors of any form of childhood abuse. Offers a helpline, email support and local services.

SUPPORT FOR SURVIVORS
Telephone: 0115 962 2722
Email: hello@supportforsurvivors.org
Website: https://supportforsurvivors.org
Support for adult survivors of child abuse.

DOMESTIC ABUSE

THE DASH CHARITY
Telephone: 0175 354 9865
Website: https://thedashcharity.org.uk
Information, a helpline, advocacy services and legal support for adults who have experienced domestic abuse. Also runs refuge accommodation in Berkshire for women and children.

ONE IN FOUR
Telephone: 0800 121 7114
Website: https://oneinfour.org.uk
Offers advocacy services, counselling and resources for adults who have experienced trauma, domestic or sexual abuse in childhood.

SAFER PLACES
Telephone: 0330 102 5811
Website: https://www.saferplaces.co.uk
Helpline, a live chat and information service for adults who have experienced domestic and sexual abuse or violence. Offers refuge accommodation services in Essex and Hertfordshire.

DOMESTIC ABUSE SUPPORT FOR BAME PEOPLE

ASHIANA

Telephone: 0114 255 5740

Website: www.ashianasheffield.org

Supports Black, Asian, Minority Ethnic and refugee women in England who have experienced domestic abuse, forced marriage and honour-based violence. Also supports children and young people.

ROSHINI

Telephone: 0800 953 9666 (domestic abuse)

Telephone: 0800 953 9777 (forced marriage and honour-based abuse)

Website: https://www.roshnibirmingham.org.uk

Supports people from BAME communities who have experienced domestic abuse, honour-based violence, forced marriage, rape or sexual assault. Offers two 24-hour multilingual helplines – national support for domestic abuse, and support in the West Midlands for forced marriage and honour-based abuse.

SOUTHALL BLACK SISTERS
Telephone: 0208 571 9595
Website: https://southallblacksisters.org.uk
Information, advice, advocacy, practical help, counselling and support to BAME women and children who have experienced domestic and sexual violence. Offers telephone services in multiple languages. Operates within the London Borough of Ealing.

VICTIM SUPPORT OF MULTIPLE FORMS OF ABUSE

VICTIM SUPPORT
Website: https://www.victimfocus.org.uk
Dedicated to challenging poor practice, discrimination and oppression of victims of abuse, trauma and violence.

Working to change the way professionals and the public understand, perceive and discuss victims of abuse, trauma and violence.

Influencing governments, policymakers, practitioners, academics and the public to treat victims with respect and compassion.